VIGILANTE
SHERIFF

VIGILANTE
SHERIFF

The Truth about
Corrupt Prosecutors
Weaponizing the
Legal System

Victor Hill

ISBN: 979-8-9913595-0-4 - Paperback
eISBN: 979-8-9913595-1-1 - eBook

Library of Congress Control Number: 2024917158

⊗This paper meets the requirements of ANSI/NISO Z39.48-1992 (Permanence of Paper)

090924

This book is dedicated to the inmates at the Forest City Federal Corrections Institute where I am now a prisoner as I write. I thought this prison would become my monastery so I could engage in long hours of meditation. But to my surprise, this prison has become my university, and the inmates my professors. I never planned to write a book. This book was their idea and their requirement as my "dissertation" to earn an honorary doctoral degree from their university. My "professors" contributed a lot to the content of what you are about to read and checked daily on my progress. No formal education from an accredited university can match the honorary doctorate in criminal justice I received from them. I will be forever indebted to all of them for helping me achieve "higher education."

"This is the lesson: never give in, never give in, never, never, never, never—in nothing, great or small, large or petty—never give in except to convictions of honor and good sense. Never yield to force; never yield to the apparently overwhelming might of the enemy."

—Winston Churchill

Contents

Introduction

The American English Collins Dictionary defines the word *vigilante* as "a person who violently and summarily takes the law into their own hands to avenge crimes without recourse to lawful procedures."

I am Victor Hill, and I am the former sheriff of Clayton County. I am also the first African American to serve as sheriff in the history of Clayton County. I am not known for being the county's first African American sheriff. I am known for being the toughest sheriff on crime in the county's history and lowering the violent crime rate that was plaguing "my county." I am probably even better known for being able to prevent and control the violence in the Clayton County Jail. "My jail" became known as the toughest para-military jail in Georgia. Sheriffs from across the state would call me when they had violent inmates they could not control and ask me to house them for the safety of their staff. Foreign officials who toured my jail invited me to Africa, Israel, and Haiti, and a documentary crew from England flew down to discuss having me fly to England to do a docuseries on how to fix and control their jails.

At a homeowner's meeting I attended after I had my deputies remove a drug house from their community, a citizen referred to me as "the crime fighter." That nickname stuck and would become a brand that kept me reelected. That brand was inspired by my likeness to perhaps the most famous fictional vigilante of all time because of our similar origins, as if life was imitating art.

Gangster rappers, both underground and famous, began mentioning me in their lyrics. A *Grand Theft Auto* gamer added my patrol car with my name on it to chase the *GTA* bad guys. When the Atlanta riots became uncontrollable, the Atlanta police chief called for my team and I to come and stop it. And stop it we did, without losing a single patrol car in the flames as did all of the other responding agencies. The *Atlanta Voice* did an article titled "Gangs are leaving Clayton County Courtesy of Victor Hill," adding a video interview of a gangster disciple—who kept his identity from being shown—describing explicitly how he felt I had run all the gangs out of Clayton County.

Even though I had already long since angered the media and continued to do so by not granting them any interviews for well over a decade, they admitted in this article the crime had decreased and cited an 8 percent drop in the murder rate. The article went on to say that though many did not agree with my unorthodox methods, the results were numerically undeniable and lawful. Put this together with all the social media memes that popped up anytime an atrocious crime occurred that fans and foes alike thought I would be "the right one" to quell it, and thus the urban myth of a perceived *Vigilante Sheriff* was created.

In May 2020, the day after I was reelected to my fourth term in office, the FBI came to my office with a search warrant. I was not alarmed because what crime could they possibly have on me? For a long time, they would not tell me why they were there. Then one of them slipped and said a name, and I instantly knew it was a politically motivated move by the Clayton County District Attorney and her friends who just tried to unseat me in the 2020 election. The agents finally said they were there to investigate the use of the safety restraint chair. Interestingly, though the total number of uses of the safety restraint chair by my staff totaled over six hundred times, they were only interested in the few times I authorized its use. Once they got the reports of inmates I ordered the use of the restraint chair on, they contacted them and told them their civil rights were violated and asked if they felt any "pain" while they were restrained. Despite the facts that none of these inmates were touched or injured, checked on every fifteen minutes by nurses and staff that was logged, and the sheriff's office policy backed by approved training from the Georgia Public Safety Training Center justified my use of the safety restraint chair as a preventative measure, I was indicted a year later by the feds for violating seven inmates' constitutional rights.

Lynsey Barron, a defense attorney who is a former federal prosecutor in the Atlanta office that had me indicted, read the indictments and found it odd I had been indicted for only authorizing violent offenders to be restrained in the safety restraint chair for safety. Barron found a way to get in touch with me and said that the whole time she had been in the US attorney's office and prosecuted cases related to the restraint chair, she had never seen such a prosecution. Barron went on to say that in the cases they prosecuted related to the restraint chair, there was always some type of violence that was done to the inmates after they were restrained. That did not occur in my case. Barron also told me she had researched the matter and nowhere in any circuit of the country had any law enforcement official ever been prosecuted or even held civilly liable for only authorizing inmates to be placed in a restraint chair for safety. Barron added that the Constitution forbids the prosecution of anyone for a crime, that there is no established case law precedent, therefore prosecutors were actually violating *my* constitutional rights while claiming they were protecting the rights of the inmates. Although I had already obtained counsel, Barron felt so strongly about my case, she volunteered pro bono to help represent me against her former colleagues boldly and publicly, calling my charges "a novel theory of prosecution."

Barron filed a motion to have the case dismissed noting that the US marshals kept inmates in restraints any time she would interview clients as a preventative safety measure for hours at a time. The motion and her oral arguments clearly articulated I should have never been charged and that the prosecutors had other civil options to challenge our policy and training if that was truly their concern. Everyone thought this motion would be the end of it and put this to rest because case law states cases that are not clearly defined by law should not go before a jury. But it would not be that simple because this case had nothing to do with protecting inmates' constitutional rights or the use of a safety restraint chair. We must never forget that even if the feds are involved, all politics is still local.

Baron had no idea she was entering a tangled web of politics that spun back to 2005 when I was first elected sheriff, removing an "old guard" administration and replacing it with my own. This made me an enemy of the Clayton County DA who had indicted me ten years ago under the RICO act, as payback and a way to keep me out of office. The Clayton DA used the RICO act, which was designed to go after organized crime, to allege that every time I drove my assigned vehicle out of town and put gas in it (even though I was on call 24/7) was "theft of a motor vehicle," making me the culprit of a "criminal enterprise." This attempt failed with my acquittal but left a bitter taste in the DA's mouth.

Barron also did not know the lead investigator for the politically motivated RICO case I was acquitted from was now on the FBI task force and was leading the restraint chair investigation at the behest of the Clayton County DA, who was trying to give the appearance that her hands were clean this time. Barron did not know the federal judge assigned to my case was married to a former prosecutor working in the Clayton County DA's office during my RICO indictment and is also a friend of the Clayton County DA. And Barron did not know the federal judge was also Facebook friends with one of my political opponents who took this contrived opportunity to run for sheriff again. Not only would this federal judge refuse to dismiss the case and refuse to let us bring out all of the incestuous relationships with the Clayton DA's Office at trial, but this judge would later coerce a jury that stayed hung for four days to a guilty verdict calling a holdout juror and questioning him in front of the media and public twice. Something that has never been done in federal court history. As a result of all this collaborative effort, I became the first law-enforcement official in the history of the United States to be federally prosecuted and sent to prison for authorizing the use of the safety restraint chair. A "crime" for which no one had ever been prosecuted for in the history of federal prosecution and a "crime" for which there was no established criminal or civil law (see reference in the appendix of other egregious cases never criminally prosecuted).

This book is not just about the details and exposing a politically motivated prosecution. This book is the whole story of why and how I became the sheriff of Clayton County. It is about fighting crime and why my team and I became the most effective crime fighters in recent Georgia law enforcement history. This book is about the truth of what works to prevent and control crime on the streets and in our nation's uncontrollable and dangerous jails within the lawful confines of the Constitution. It is also about why what is being done now doesn't work, and never will.

But this book is also a huge dichotomy because I am also going to articulate the other side of the perspective of how inmates are really being victimized by our criminal justice system. I am here with them now. They have opened up to me, I have listened, and their perspective needs to be told here as well. They have read and contributed to my appeal to the eleventh circuit. It was their idea I write this book, hoping someone would pay attention. I am just as motivated to speak for them as I am to speak out and say what law enforcement officials are afraid to say due to their fear of the media—and their very understandable fear of rogue media-hungry prosecutors. Those prosecutors who will "Monday morning quarterback" law enforcement officials' every deed to come up with "novel theories of prosecution," hoping to achieve fifteen seconds of fame at press conferences or to force a political agenda under the guise they are just enforcing the law.

So here it is, uncut and unadulterated from the proverbial horse's mouth that has not granted an interview to the media in over a decade. And when this book is said and done, I will leave it to the reader to conclude whether I am the vigilante that prosecutors needed to protect violent criminals from, or if the real vigilantes we all need protection from are the prosecutors who are allowed to commit perjury to grand juries with impunity, violating the very same Constitution they claim to uphold.

Chapter 1

Life Imitates Art

As a teenager, I was an avid reader of comic books. I didn't really pay much attention to Batman comics because I had only seen a version of Batman portrayed on TV starring Adam West from the sixties that gave me the false impression that Batman was just a kiddie character with harmless kiddie villains—like the Joker, who was portrayed as a robber who cracked jokes. I had no idea that TV had modified the characters for political reasons. I also had no idea that my limited knowledge of this fictional vigilante character was not only going to change my opinion of him, but it was also going to change the course of my life.

One day, while at a convenience store in the neighborhood I grew up in, James Island, South Carolina, I was going through a comic book rack looking for a good one to read. A comic book titled *The Dark Knight*, with an ominous drawing of the Batman, captured my attention. This comic book contained Batman's origin, which I did not know was so dark and grim. Allow me to paraphrase in a short summary.

When Batman was a child, he and his parents took a shortcut down a back alley while leaving the theater. A robber stepped out of the shadows, demanding money and valuables while holding his parents and him at gunpoint. The robber tried to snatch a pearl necklace from his mother's neck, manhandling and choking her in the process. His father, as any man would, stepped up to defend his wife, demanding the robber take his hands off her. The robber gunned him down in cold blood in front of his wife and child. As Batman's father fell to the ground, bleeding profusely, his mother began to scream. The robber then gunned down Batman's mother to silence her screams, leaving him as a child orphan who had to watch his parents bleed to death. The psychological trauma that incurred from seeing his parents murdered before his eyes resulted in a vow to not only find this criminal, but to pursue all criminals who commit the ultimate theft for which there can be no restitution, the theft of a human life. And thus, the Batman, who became the dreaded creature of the night that would protect his city from the domestic terrorism of crime, was born.

As I began to read more and more, I also found out the Joker was not just a kiddie villain that cracked jokes but was a psychotic serial killer who was born from the trauma of a "bad day" he had in life, that was well articulated in the acclaimed *Killing Joke* comic book. The fictional conflict between the Batman and the Joker reached the level of such a psychological thriller, it resulted in a whole book being written and dedicated to the psychology of the trauma which put them in a lifetime conflict with each other. I became a captivated fan and read Batman comic books often to keep up with his exploits, especially when one featured the Joker. I could have never predicted that in a very grim twist of fate, my life would imitate the art that was just a pastime for reading.

It all started when a friend I had known since the first grade did not show up at home after getting off from a part-time after-school job. For days, the absence went unexplained. Ironically as fate would have it, the body of that friend was found behind the very same convenience store I had read *The Dark Knight* comic book. It was a brutal murder that entailed sexual assault, mutilation, and dismemberment. Once the details of this murder came out, fear spread quickly through the neighborhood like stage-four cancer.

Just like all politics is local, all crime is local as well. In our community lived a well-known and decorated homicide detective who had solved the most unsolved murders in the history of the Charleston County Police Force, named Eugene Frazier. Our community is also where the suspects who were responsible for this brutal and savage murder lived. All of us lived within a six-block radius. It would be now-retired Lieutenant Eugene Frazier who would solve the murder, identify the suspects, and track them down to justice, restoring calm to a community paralyzed in fear.

This murder would become the catalyst that fueled my desire to pursue law enforcement—not as a career, but as a passion. But not just any type of law enforcement. Law enforcement is very diverse and there are many types of cops. There are traffic cops, probation cops, beat cops, drug cops, state and federal cops, and the list goes on and on. My intent was very specific. I wanted to pursue the worst thieves known to man: those who stole lives. I wanted to be the hunter who hunted the killers. Years later when I became a homicide detective, I sought out retired Lieutenant Frazier to be my "sensei" in the art of solving murders.

When I was a senior in high school, the police chief of Charleston City came to my social studies class to speak to us. There were only about nineteen of us in the classroom, so it was a very personal setting where we got to ask questions. It wasn't just any police chief, it was Ruben Greenberg, a law-enforcement legend. He was also notably the first and only African American chief Charleston City ever had. With the history of Charleston being a major part of the slave trade in America, that was and still is interesting, but there was a whole lot more to him than just being the first African American to lead the Charleston City Police. Reuben Greenberg was a pioneer in unorthodox, effective crime fighting. He successfully reduced the crime rate in Charleston City to the point where some began referring to the once crime-ridden violent city as "Saintsville." He was tough on crime, and he ruled with an iron fist. Our class didn't have a lot of questions for the police chief, but I did. His speech kept me captivated. His theories and strategies as to how he approached controlling and preventing crime had me spellbound. At that moment, I was sold. I not only knew what I was going to be but under whose leadership it would happen.

When I graduated from high school, I found a job working at an ice cream parlor in downtown Charleston. Police officers on foot patrol would stop in daily and I would engage them with a barrage of questions, making it known I was going to become a recruit as soon as I turned twenty-one.

One day, a police captain happened to stop into the parlor and when I told him my interest, he told me about a police cadet program I could join instantly at eighteen years old. It turned out Chief Reuben Greenberg had created a program where cadets could work full time, mainly doing parking enforcement, until they're old enough to become certified police officers. The captain told me it would be a great way to get started early and get as close to on-the-job training as I could until I became of age. My application went in the next day. Within three months, I got the job. It was the best move I could have made. In retrospect, it was the only move I could have made because it was a move that would unfold my destiny.

Chapter 2

Charleston City Police

I s there such a thing as an indispensable man?

It was 1983, the year I graduated from high school, when I joined the Charleston City police force. I had no clue how fortunate I was to be under the leadership of a man who was and remains a legendary figure in law enforcement. You really can't measure anything until you have something to measure it against. It has been said that a leader and those he leads will never know how well he has led until he is gone. No one can truly gauge how good or how bad the leadership of any organization is until you get to work under the leadership of other leaders. But I can give you a clue on how to gauge any leadership, and that is to look at the bottom line of their results. Results tell us everything about a leader. In corporate America, the bottom line is whether the business is profitable or not because their stock is either going down or going up. So it is in the world of law enforcement. The crime is either going up or it's going down and the direction of the crime tells you a lot about the direction of the sheriff or the chief. It's just that simple. You can also tell a lot when a chief or sheriff is confronted with a rising crime rate. If they start blaming crime on Covid-19, or a rising murder rate on domestic violence they claim no one can control, that is an indicator their leadership is excuse-driven. Excuse-driven leadership in law enforcement always results in higher crime. The excuse syndrome that plagues many of our leaders was never the case with the leadership of Chief Ruben Greenberg.

Chief Ruben Greenberg was always on the cutting edge of how to effectively and efficiently fight crime. He was light years ahead of the game on how to bring proven results that could be felt. His crime reduction methodology was so intriguing and revered, he was invited to numerous national talk shows and was even featured on *60 Minutes*. He wrote a book titled *Let's Take Back Our Streets*, which is still light years ahead of our community policing scholars of today.

What really made Greenberg stand out was that he was a front-line leader. Greenberg went out on patrol almost daily, so it was not unusual to hear him come across the police radio while working the streets. Not only would he go out on patrol in his squad car, he would also occasionally go on foot patrol, but not always necessarily on foot. Chief Greenberg loved to roller skate. So, when he would do foot patrol, sometimes he would do it on skates instead. One night, he just happened to be in the area where a burglary was taking place and joined in on the "foot" pursuit while on skates and captured the suspect. That incident became legend, and the story has been told a million times, a million ways, transforming it into urban legend form.

Another of the many things that Greenberg was known for was the legendary units he created. He had created the Flying Squad, named after the famous Flying Squad in England. He spoke about his Flying Squad when he came to my high school and spoke to my class. I was intrigued and remembered asking him why they were called the Flying Squad. I'll never forget his answer. He said the men he assigned to that squad were men who had the ability to run like they were flying, so they could catch any criminal who attempted to flee capture. At that moment, I aspired to be on his Flying Squad. But there was another unit he created I found much more intriguing once I was on the force, his Tac Squad.

The Tac Squad was a plain-clothes patrol unit that would patrol the streets just like regular uniform patrol, but in plain clothes and in undercover cars that blended in. This was common sense, cutting-edge policing that enabled them to catch many crimes in progress. This unit would drive any type of car, from Buick Regals to Chevy Camaros. They were known on the street sometimes as the Jump-Out Squad because, sometimes, they would ride four to a car and when they pulled up on thugs that had taken over street corners, all four doors opened, and they would jump out causing shock and awe among criminals.

But they did so much more than occasional jump-out missions. This unit was the epitome of what is now referred to by law enforcement scholars as "problem-solving policing." The real reason they were called the Tac Squad was because they were tasked with coming up with tactical solutions to whatever crime problems were taxing the city. For instance, if there was a neighborhood where a lot of bicycles were stolen, they would target that area by placing a bicycle where the potential for it to be stolen was high. Some of them would be on a roof, watching through binoculars, while others were blending into the environment, perhaps disguised as a drunk on a park bench. When the thief would show up and steal the bicycle, he would be unpleasantly surprised when five to eight men he thought were just street people would suddenly converge on him—especially when he thought he was about to get away with an easy theft. The Tac Squad was a very effective unit, and they were one of the main tools Greenberg used to clean up the streets of Charleston. They made a name for themselves in the streets and were feared by the criminal element of which many left our jurisdiction because they simply could not operate with them around. Greenberg kept his agency up to date on the latest equipment and the most effective tactics. He led us to do effective police work, focusing only on what worked to control and reduce crime.

At eighteen years of age, all of this was exciting to watch. I could not wait to turn twenty-one to become a police officer. All I did was work night and day toward that goal—even during my extracurricular activities. If I was not reading books on how to solve crimes, like the thousand-page volume *Fundamentals of Criminal Investigations*, I was working on earning a black belt in martial arts so I would be able to handle myself against anyone, regardless of their size and strength.

During that time as a police cadet, mainly doing parking enforcement, I occasionally got to do some real police work. Sometimes, I would just happen to be in the right place at the right time when a crime would go out across the radio, and I would spot the suspect. I would always follow them and call it across the police radio until the patrolman could respond to arrest them. One time this happened with a shoplifter, and the police chief himself responded. After it was over, he called me across the radio to meet him just to tell me I did a good job. For an eighteen-year-old who was just starting to explore his destiny, that more than made my day and inspired me to find as many criminals as I could while doing parking enforcement just so the chief would send me to the academy the minute I turned twenty-one. It worked!

One day, I was in a break room, reading over the *Fundamentals of Criminal Investigation* (I carried that book around the same way my dearly departed mother used to carry her Bible.) Chief Greenberg just happened to walk in, and when he saw the thickness of the book, he asked me what I was reading. When I told him, he smiled and said, "Good, because I'm getting ready to send you to the academy next month."

I had not turned twenty-one yet, but I would by the time I graduated from the academy. "Thank you, Chief!" I said.

Chief Greenberg knew I was actively practicing martial arts and joked as he parted, saying, "I know you're into all of the kung fu, but make sure you become proficient with the Smith & Wesson," and chuckled before he walked off.

"Yes sir," I responded. I immediately found a way to start learning how to gunfight as well. I did not want to disappoint him, or myself, and I was determined to be the best in the business.

Once I went to the police academy and graduated, I was assigned to the Team Two Patrol District. For those not familiar with Charleston, South Carolina, Team Two encompasses the area people from all over the world come to see to take tours of the slave market, and mansions owned by the rich during the Civil War that are still occupied overlooking the Charleston harbor. But the Team Two Patrol District was a huge dichotomy. At that time, Calhoun Street was a distinct line between wealth and poverty, and safety and violence. It was truly a diverse area to patrol because one moment you could be taking a report from a millionaire in the living room of his mansion and as soon as you get in your car, you could be responding to a shooting or a stabbing at the projects on Concord Street.

This patrol district brought the skill of being able to "walk with Kings—nor lose to common touch," as articulated by Rudyard Kipling in his famous poem "If." This was a great training ground because a good cop should be able to go to a trap house and address crackheads in a language they clearly understand, and then put on a suit and tie the next day and fly to Washington to address Congress in a language they can understand as well.

I learned a lot on this patrol beat, but most importantly, I got to see an effective leader in action. I can recall pulling over a car on a traffic stop at three in the morning and taking a gun off a suspect while calling for backup. The first car to pull up to back me up was Chief Ruben Greenberg. I can also recall getting into a foot pursuit with a drug dealer in the Concord projects and the first car that skidded up to help me catch the suspect was Chief Greenberg. At that time, he was the only chief I had ever worked for, so I thought this was the norm, but I was witnessing a rare and effective style of frontline leadership I would never see anything come remotely close to again.

Shoot on Sight

To further illustrate just how tough Chief Greenberg was on crime and how much he had control of the streets, I need only speak of when a serial rapist began to terrorize Charleston. After several women were raped and investigations had been ongoing, detectives finally came up with a break and identified the serial rapist. But the rapist was not in custody and was still at large.

Chief Greenberg put the picture of the suspect out at a press conference, telling the public that the suspect was being searched for and that he was not going to rape anyone anymore because he had given his police officers orders to shoot on sight if the suspect tried to escape capture by fleeing. The next day, the rapist turned himself in at police headquarters, walking in with his hands up.

To the "woke" critics of today, what Chief Greenberg did would be politically incorrect and political prosecutors looking to make a case would say it was unconstitutional since the rapist was not even a "pretrial detainee" yet. But to the contrary, Greenberg's orders were within the confines of training and law that still exist today. Whether you liked his methods or not, Charleston was a safe place to be under his leadership, and most citizens appreciated his efforts to keep the city of Charleston safe, as the majority of Clayton County citizens appreciated my efforts to keep "my county" safe, which they showed by electing me to office four times.

Greenberg's leadership truly shaped how I policed the streets of Clayton County. He was an amazing man to work for. But I have to be honest and admit I did not appreciate it at the time I worked for him. Like a son who does not appreciate his strict father until he is thrust out into the world with children of his own, so it was with my law-enforcement father. It would take me working for three other agencies before I went on to become sheriff when I developed a deep appreciation and undying admiration for this man. Greenberg was not an easy man to work for, especially if you were undisciplined or lazy. He ran a very tight ship and used certain military standards to keep everything in order. Chief Greenberg was the epitome of the leadership philosophy of inspecting which you expect. He had yearly inspections where we would all stand at attention for inspections of our uniforms, weapons, and equipment. Supervisors were required to inspect officers before they went on the road at every roll call. And if you just happened to run into Chief Greenberg while walking down the hall, he might inadvertently stop and check your weapon for cleanliness or your uniform and equipment to make sure you were up to his professional standards.

Also, his discipline was very strict. I can remember lots of officers standing outside his office, waiting to see how many days of suspension they were getting for violation of policies and procedures. Chief Greenberg handed out suspensions, demotions, and terminations like the Easter Bunny handed out candy. I must admit I thought his discipline was too harsh and resented it as so many others did. I eventually went to work for a neighboring agency because I thought I would like it better. I did not. It turned out I greatly missed the order, structure, and high standards from my first law enforcement job. But even more, I missed seeing and feeling the results of a consistent decline in crime.

Try as they might, no one in the state of South Carolina could deny that Charleston Police was the most effective law enforcement in the state at that time, and the numbers did not lie about the crime reduction. However, very few employees—including myself—did not want to admit the reason we were so effective was because Chief Greenberg was consistent about disciplining and removing ineffective employees. It was not until I worked for three other agencies where there was no discipline that I came to the startling realization their dysfunction came from retaining dysfunctional, nonperforming employees because no one had the balls to remove them. Running a law enforcement agency is not an easy task and, in some ways, it is like running a kindergarten where all of the kids have guns. Not only do you have to keep control of the hardened criminals on the streets and in jail, but if you don't keep the people under your command in line, they can and will run rogue very easily. Even worse, they will simply shortcut or not do their jobs to get as close to a free paycheck as possible. It's hard to find parents who don't say they now understand what their parents were trying to do once they have children of their own. Years later, I would have that same conversation with my "law-enforcement father" after I became sheriff.

Greenberg was the police chief of Charleston, South Carolina, for twenty-three years. He was still chief when I was elected sheriff and honored me by coming to my swearing-in. He was the first, and only, African American police chief in the history of Charleston, South Carolina. After his passing, I read an interesting editorial about him in the Charleston *Post and Courier*, asking the proverbial question: Is there such a thing as an indispensable man? I must say, after having the honor of working for him and working for other law-enforcement leaders, the answer is unequivocally yes. I have come to learn, after thirty years in this game, everything rises and falls on leadership. It has been said that an army of sheep led by a lion will always defeat an army of lions led by sheep. The Charleston Police Department has never been the same since he's been gone. No one has ever regained control over the crime in the streets like Greenberg did, and no one probably ever will.

Chapter 3

Clayton County Police

W hen I moved to Atlanta, it was with the intention of joining the Atlanta Police Department. The specialized unit they had that was in the ballpark of types of units I had grown accustomed to in Charleston under Chief Greenberg was their R.E.D.D.O.G. unit—Run Every Drug Dealer Out of Georgia. I figured getting on that unit would be a great start until I could get on to the homicide unit, which was known back then as the Hat Squad. But the wait to get on with APD back then was long and Clayton County Police picked me up first, so I went there with the idea I would do a year or two there and then go to APD.

July 20, 1992, is the date I joined the Clayton County Police Department. At that time, I was one of only sixteen black police officers on the entire police force. One of the black police officers out of sixteen who was there when I joined was Jeff Turner, who is now the sitting Chairman of Clayton County. Turner, at that time, was a property detective. There were two weeks before the new hires and I would be sent to the academy, so we were assigned to ride with different detectives for a week. As fate would have it, I spent a day riding with Turner not knowing I was meeting a man who would become my nemesis and stalker over the course of my thirty-year career in Clayton County. Turner was behind on his paperwork for a case review and contacting victims of theft cases assigned to him so the first three hours of the ride-along were spent catching up on what should have already been done. The rest of the day was spent going to the mall, walking around, and visiting his friends. We did absolutely no police work. I remember thinking how pusillanimous Turner was as a detective and would have been in a state of shock if I was told he would one day become the chief of police and the chairman of Clayton County, which is a position the equivalent of being mayor. The pusillanimous qualities of performance he displayed that day I was assigned to ride with him would remain consistent with the lackluster performance the county would receive from him as the police chief and with him at the helm as the chairman. Turner had problems getting promoted and when he failed promotional tests, he would complain that the exams were racially designed to keep him and other black officers from getting promoted. That was a lie. He just did not have the aptitude to pass the test. Turner kept filing lawsuits and got thrown promotions to shut him up and make it go away. He then became the affirmative action poster child of the Clayton County Police Department, and even though it was obvious he could not find a prostitute in a prostitution house or command a playground fight, the administration would continue to throw him a promotion anytime one became available for the next higher rank. Perhaps this was done because of the explosive growth of African Americans moving into the county and the, at that time, predominantly white administration's fear of being labeled as racist. It was a mistake. If you look at the condition of the county today, it is the direct result of Turner's weak, pusillanimous leadership as the chairman for the last twelve years.

Clayton County was a very different place back then with the demographics being the exact opposite of what it is now. It was a very quiet bedroom community. Areas like Mount Zion Boulevard were mostly just wooded areas around and across from Home Depot. There were still a lot of rural farm-like properties on the south side of the county, and a few remain to this day. Back then, the north side of Clayton County had an unusual amount of apartment complexes, but they were very nice and expensive. Most of them were in the Garden Walk Boulevard area and were occupied by pilots, airline stewardesses, and airport employees. However, being a cop there at that time was very routine and I was bored out of my mind. Clayton County was a low-crime area where people, mostly white and some black, moved to get away from the urban crime and chaos that was in the city of Atlanta. But this would take a 180-degree turn no one saw coming. It all was about to change, and changed fast, in just four short years after my arrival.

What became a great historical moment for the city of Atlanta became an urban nightmare for the leaders in Clayton County who were mostly white at that time. In 1996, Clayton County would make a huge demographic shift that would forever change the direction of the county's future. When the Olympics came to Atlanta, a lot of the inner-city population was relocated to different areas to make room for the venue in Atlanta. Vouchers for Section 8 homes and apartments became plentiful, and Clayton had the number of apartments to fill them. The vouchers for Section 8 filled rapidly in Clayton County, and as a result, Clayton began to experience what is referred to as "white flight," causing a rapid demographic flip as more urban African Americans from

Atlanta fluctuated into the county. This became a huge challenge for the predominant white leadership in the county. Add to this challenge that the majority of the police force was white. This shift brought inner-city urban crime that the Clayton County Police Force and its leaders were simply not prepared to handle at the time.

What was their nightmare, I must confess, was my opportunity. This was the challenge I had come to Atlanta for. The year before the Olympics, I was promoted to be a Robbery-Homicide Detective and became a Hostage Negotiator. The timing could not have been more perfect, because the boredom I was experiencing when I first got to Clayton County was quickly coming to an end and the years of physical and mental training I had subjected myself to were for a time such as this. The whole time I'd been in law enforcement, my goal was to work homicides. This was my true reason for relocating to Atlanta to begin with, but now there was no longer any need to leave Clayton County to go to Atlanta, because Atlanta had now come to Clayton County.

I would go on to spend a decade as a Robbery-Homicide Detective and Hostage Negotiator in Clayton County as the county changed and grew more and more violent. The ten years I spent tracking robbers and killers or conducting negotiations to talk them out and surrender could be a novel all its own. But in this book, I will just briefly describe what it was like to be the only black homicide detective at a time when the county had rapidly turned African American.

Most of the members of the Clayton County Police Department from the top to the bottom, including the sixteen black officers, were used to patrolling the county when it was more rural, sub-urban, and mostly Caucasian. Now, the department was faced with urban gangs that brought crimes like home invasion robberies and drive-by shootings. Many of the Clayton County patrolmen who worked there at that time did so because they did not want to deal with that type of urban crime. It very quickly became obvious that they not only did not know how to handle it, but they did not even understand it.

Let me give a small, comical example:

Often, when we were interrogating suspects in shootings, rob-beries, or murders, I would have to translate what was being said to a lot of the officers who were in no way familiar with the culture or slang of the streets. It kind of reminded me of the sitcom *Sanford and Son*, where the black cop had to translate to Fred Sanford what the white cop was trying to say, and then translate to the white cop what Fred Sanford was saying. As funny as those skits were, they were very true representations of art imitating life. For example, I remember one time I was interrogating an informant who began telling me who was hitting "licks" on Riverdale Road. After I got through talking to him, the supervisor asked me what a "lick" was. When I told him it was a robbery, he was quite surprised and looked confused. This is just a small example of the huge cultural adjustment it took for officers and the leadership who were used to patrolling a mostly rural county with a different demographic. Now, they were suddenly dealing with a group of people they simply did not understand.

But the problem was much deeper than that. The Clayton County Police Department ran as a response agency only. The county police simply responded to 911 calls and handled the aftermath of it. There was nothing being done proactively to prevent and control crime. If it was a murder or robbery, detectives responded after the fact to see if it could be solved with no real pressure to do so unless it was political. There were no units designed to prevent or interfere with robberies in progress and there were no strategies in place with innovative ways to prevent and control the number of killings that were increasingly taking place.

When I would go back home to visit my mother and grand-mother, I would always stop and visit Lieutenant Eugene Frazier to go over the homicides I was working on to get tips on how to solve them, and of course, I would visit Chief Rueben Greenberg. One visit home was very different and very special. When I stopped by Chief Greenberg's office to say hi one afternoon, he told me he was going on patrol that night and asked me if I would like to tag along. Of course, the answer was yes. Later that evening, I met him in front of the police headquarters and got in his car, and out on patrol we went. What he would say and show me that night would set the course of what I would ultimately do in Clayton County. I will never forget it.

We were approaching Ashley Avenue and Nunan Street when he started asking me questions. The first question was, "What do you hear on the radio?"

I responded, "Sir, I'm not sure what you mean."

He then asked slightly differently, "What have you been hearing on the police radio since you've been riding with me?" I was still not sure how to answer the question. He then asked, "What are you hearing on the radio right now?"

I listened and said, "Sir, I'm not hearing anything on the radio. It's rather quiet."

He said, "Exactly! When you were here, do you remember how active the radio was on a Friday night?"

"Yes, sir, I do remember," I replied.

Greenberg said, "You know why the radio is so quiet now?"

I replied, "No, sir, please explain."

"Because I ran all the criminals out of the city." He pointed and said, "Look at that corner right there. Who do you see hanging out there?"

"No one, sir," I said.

"Exactly. If you remember, there used to be about anywhere from eight to fifteen guys standing on that corner, correct?"

"Yes, you are right," I responded in awe.

He said, "Who do you see there now?"

I laughed and said, "No one, sir."

The chief then said, "That's because they're all either in jail or I ran them out of town."

I sat in silence, totally amazed for a minute because I couldn't believe what I was hearing and seeing. I was captivated. It almost sounded too good to be true, but there it was before my eyes and seeing is definitely believing. I remember thinking to myself, *Now, this is real effective police work the community can see and feel. Someone needs to do this in Clayton County.* And at that moment, I knew that someone was going to be me.

Greenberg did not know it, but he had just written my campaign speech I would use at every political forum to be elected sheriff. It went like this:

"When the settlers moved out West, they did so because they saw great opportunities for themselves and their families to have a better quality of life. But the West also attracted outlaws who saw their own opportunities as well. So, what did those settlers do about it? When they went to the polls, they elected sheriffs like Pat Garrett, Wild Bill Hitchcock, and Bat Madison, because they knew they needed sheriffs who were strong enough to confront the outlaws and run them out of town. Just like the Old West, Clayton County had a lot of settlers move out here because they saw opportunities and a better quality of life for their families. But just like the Old West, Clayton County has also attracted outlaws. Let's learn from those settlers and elect a sheriff who's strong enough to confront the outlaws and run them out of town. And I respectfully submit to you that I am that man."

The community loved it, they were sold, and I was elected on the promise I would run all the outlaws out of town. And that is exactly what I did.

Chapter 4

The Office of Sheriff

B efore there were the police, before there were marshals, and way before there ever were any state and federal agencies like the GBI, FBI, or DEA, the office of sheriff existed. Indeed, the origin of the office of sheriff proceeds all and any law enforcement known to man. It is the most ancient historical law enforcement agency in the history of this planet. So ancient, so historical, that in the King James Version of the Bible, in the book of Daniel, in the third chapter and the third verse, seated in the presence of King Nebuchadnezzar is the sheriff. This is why any time politicians or media accuse the sheriff's office of duplicating the services of the police, it is comical ignorance. Think about it. How can the sheriff's office that existed before the police and any other law-enforcement agency known to man duplicate them when the sheriff's office existed before them all? All of them are in actuality duplicating the duties and function of the sheriff's office.

How fitting and fascinating that the sheriff would be mentioned in the third chapter and the third verse of Daniel, because according to our state Constitution, the sheriff has a "trinity" of duties. The sheriff is the chief jailer, the chief officer of the court, and last but certainly not least, the chief law enforcer of the county. Put a pin on that, because nowhere in the Constitution does it say two out of three, or one out of three, it says *all* three. Also, put a pin in this, the law also states that the sheriff has "a duty to protect." There is no other law enforcement agency the law says this about. So, this means if an elected sheriff does not use the office for the law-enforcement purpose of protecting the public, that sheriff is violating the law and his oath of office. But to the contrary, mostly in metro Atlanta counties where there exists a county police force in addition to the sheriff, some sheriffs choose to ignore the law enforcement part of the trinity of duties they are sworn to do.

Let's think about this for a moment. If you live in the metro area, in one of the eleven counties left that still has both a county police and sheriff's office, and the sheriff's office in your county does not put deputies on the street to protect you as opposed to just serving papers, if that sheriff is not using the resources that are paid by the taxpayers to protect them, he is actually violating the law. My vision for the sheriff's office in my county was to take this valuable and powerful resource that has no jurisdictional limitation within the state and use it for what it was designed and created for since the Old West, to fight crime.

My vision, in essence, was not a vision of reformation, but a vision of restoration. I simply wanted to see the sheriff's office return to its original jurisdiction, which is what taxpayers are paying for anyway. Because of the politics and insecurities of the leaders in the establishment when I took office, they would put out propaganda—with the help of the media—that I was doing something unlawful when I was following the law to the tee. Anyone opposing the sheriff from acting as a first responder is opposing the Constitution.

What really makes the office of sheriff so unique and effective is that nowhere else on the planet is the chief law enforcement officer elected by people other than the American sheriff. Police chiefs are appointed and so are Marshals, Constables, and Directors of state and federal law enforcement agencies. This is the same internationally as well. In foreign countries, the prime minister or some type of head-of-state appoints who would be the minister of police. But "only in America" do we enjoy the rights and privileges of being able to vote for who will hold the helm of law enforcement office as sheriff, to protect us instead of relying on a politician to make that decision for us. Because the sheriff is elected by the people, he only answers to the people and no other elected officials.

One of the founding fathers was quoted when they decided to create the office of sheriff that the office must be elected by the people to keep the sheriff from the "molestation of politicians." How wise and what foresight this showed, because it is usually the elected politicians who hamper law enforcement heads from doing the job effectively. But this wisdom was probably far deeper than what the founding fathers who influenced the decision to make the sheriff an elected position was even aware of. And that comes from the concept of "command and control."

Command and control is a long-known and proven military leadership concept that is a great indicator whether any war can be won, including the war on crime. The concept is that one person must be in charge for the operation to be effective and if you put more than one person in charge, it's less effective. Studies were done of wars as far back as the Napoleonic era, and they found that anytime an army with more than one General faced off with an army with one General, the army with several Generals always lost. Why? When you have more than one leader of equal authority, one is going to want to flank left and another one will want to flank right, and by the time they all build a census long enough to raise their hands and all say aye, the war is lost. But when you have one clear commander who gives the orders, knows what he's doing, and can tell the army which way the flank and what to do without argument from a group consensus, it's always going to be more effective.

This is why the sheriff being elected by the people, and only answering to them instead of answering to other elected officials, puts him in a better position to do the job unhampered, if he has the strength to do so. Only the sheriff can make decisions freely without their politics if his mission is to truly fight crime. His boss is the people who elected him, so a call from a little old lady saying there're drug dealers across the street from her house is far more important than a call from a mayor/chairman. The little old lady has so much *more* power and influence with a sheriff because she is who truly hired him. This gives a sheriff a true opportunity to truly serve the people and not worry about serving other elected officials. This is also why the sheriff's office was the best solution to fight crime in the Old West and remains the best solution to fight crime today—if the people can find a real sheriff to elect.

Many people who run for sheriff today run for it as a political office, with political objectives, as opposed to what the office was intended to do which is to fight crime. At the end of the day, even in modern times, the mission of the sheriff's office remains the same. It is still charged with confronting, hunting, and bringing outlaws to justice. But because the sheriff's office must also manage millions of dollars and decide who gets muti-million-dollar contracts for various services to jails, a lot of politicians run for the office instead of actual, real law enforcement professionals. A lot of them see the office as a steppingstone to higher political aspirations or they simply enjoy the prestige and power that comes with wearing a star badge and carrying a gun they really don't know how to use if they found themselves in an actual gunfight to protect the public. They covet and obtain the position without ever thinking or planning for what the position is intended for.

If you take the job seriously, being the sheriff today is no different than being the sheriff back in the days of the Old West. Even if you are in an area where politicians have successfully used a Jedi mind trick to regulate the sheriff down to a bailiff and jailer, the sheriff must still track down wanted fugitives, which is a dangerous art in itself. This means conducting manhunts for dangerous people who have warrants for everything from armed robbery to murder. Furthermore, as a jailer, you are responsible for dangerous individuals who have the capacity to not only kill each other inside of a jail, but to escape and wreak further havoc on the public. It's a rough and tough job that is not for the weak and faint of heart. It is not the type of job you get to walk around in a suit all day and go to committee meetings and host events in a community. But that is exactly what a lot of the individuals elected to the office of sheriff do instead of staying focused on what the actual detail of the job entails. So far, sheriffs have gotten away with this in counties where there are county police, staying oblivious to rising crime and saying crime control and reduction is not their job. The fear of prosecutors and the press is a factor in why a lot of these sheriffs do not do their jobs, but others never had the intention of doing so because they are only there for the politics of the position.

When I ran for sheriff, I ran on the promise that I would restore the sheriff's office back to its original jurisdiction, the asset the taxpayers are paying for to protect them. This angered a lot of the old guards in Clayton County, especially those at the county police where I worked. It was the standard mentality of, "this is the way we've always done things, so it's the way we should always do things," and still is very prevalent. Basically, they did not want anyone moving their cheese. But some of them honestly believed the sheriff's office was never intended to fight crime, and that the only thing the sheriff's office was supposed to do was run the jail, the courthouse, and serve warrants.

Let's think about this for a second. If Clayton County was formed in 1869, and the county police did not come into existence until the late 1940s, who protected the county back then? Of course it was the sheriff. When I ran for sheriff, people were really under the impression that the sheriff's office could not do any law enforcement and did not have the authority to do such. Everyone, including the employees of the sheriff's office, believed that sheriffs were just jailers and bailiffs, and that was all they were allowed to do. There were people who would speed past the sheriff's car because they didn't believe the sheriff had the authority to stop them. But nothing could be further from the truth.

County police officials would argue up and down and get out-right mad when they were confronted with the fact that not only could the sheriff's office do law enforcement work, but the sheriff's office actually had more authority and jurisdiction—which they should have known since they had to come to the sheriff to be deputized to give them the jurisdictional authority they need to effectively do their jobs. The police are limited in their jurisdiction. If you're a city cop, you can only have jurisdiction inside the city, and most of the cities in Clayton County are only four to five square miles. If you're a county cop, you only have jurisdiction within the county, but it's questionable if you have jurisdiction inside an incorporated city since it's incorporated. The sheriff has no such boundaries.

Because the sheriff is created by the state Constitution, he has statewide jurisdiction. This means that no matter where he is in the state of Georgia, he has full authority. Yes, a Clayton County deputy can be driving down the street in Savannah and has full authority to act as a law enforcement official. This is very crucial because criminals have no jurisdictional guidelines. Criminals don't worry about whether they are raping, robbing, or murdering in an incorporated city or an unincorporated county. But based on jurisdictional limitations of law enforcement—apart from the sheriff's office which has no jurisdictional limitations—all the other local, state, and federal cops are worried about what side of a county or city line they are standing on while criminals are not. This is another reason why the sheriff's office was and will always remain the best law enforcement entity to fight crime.

The office of the sheriff is the best structure to fight crime with the consent and will of the people, but just like anything else, the structure comes with downsides. Because the sheriff is an elected position and the qualifications are only to be at least twenty-five years old with no criminal history, any certified police officer can run for sheriff—as it should be since anyone can run for president. But the logistical problem comes in because people who work *for* the elected sheriff can support someone running *against* the sheriff or run against the sheriff they are working for. Although it is a right to support whoever you want in elected office, it is logistically impractical when the elected sheriff has people who work for him actively running against him. This has been the cause of a lot of political sabotage and media leaks which disrupt the functions of an office that is responsible for the safety of people's lives. Sheriff office employees who get politically involved in who the sheriff is going to be do so based not on who is better for the position, but who will give them the position they want at the sheriff's office. So, there's a constant battle every four years that goes beyond campaigning in the street and inside the walls of the sheriff's office that sometimes ends up being deadly—as Georgia saw in the 2000 Dekalb County sheriff's race. Even if it doesn't get to gunfire, employees will plot lawsuits, scandals, and, yes, even indictments so they can get the person out and get themselves or the person they want in.

Vision of Reform

As I said earlier, I did not reform the sheriff's office; I just restored it to its original jurisdiction. But there had to be some reformation involved in that process. I knew that for the sheriff's office to be successful in reducing the crime in Clayton County, drastic changes were going to have to be made. That drastic change included personnel. Though the sheriff's office shared the same shooting range as the police department, the standard for the Clayton County sheriff's office was different and lower than the standard for the Clayton County Police. A sheriff's deputy was allowed to carry a firearm if he could shoot 70 percent accuracy or higher while a county police officer had to shoot 80 percent or higher. It was as if the leadership at the Clayton County sheriff's office was saying it was okay to have a lower standard for deputies who were tasked with facing the same dangers and protecting the same population as county police officers, and that sheriff's deputies did not have to shoot as well as county police officers. Not only were the shooting standards lower for the sheriff's office than for the county police, but the vast majority of the sheriff's deputies at the time were not even physically capable of doing the job.

There was a lower standard for shooting and a *much* lower standard for physical fitness. Physical fitness is the oxymoron that has prevailed throughout a lot of law enforcement agencies throughout the years. We're supposed to protect the public from dangerous individuals, and the perception—at least on TV—is that cops can outrun and outfight the bad guys. But because no standards were being upheld by strong leadership, that wasn't the case at the Clayton County sheriff's office. Not only were these types of standards not being upheld, I doubt if they ever existed at all, thereby creating a weak sheriff's office that garnered no fear or respect among criminals—something needed to maintain control of the jail and courthouse as well as the streets. Even if the sheriff's only job was to protect the courthouse, with the amount of violence that happens at courthouses all over the country, you would think the caliber of deputy you would be looking for is one that should be able to shoot far better than a patrol officer, because that deputy can be called upon at any moment to defend the public or himself in a close-quarter, crowded situation inside of a courthouse setting. Instead, the culture at the Clayton County sheriff's office was to put the oldest and most out-of-shape people, who were not proficient with their firearms, at the courthouse. It was the attitude of, "Hell, it's just the courthouse. Nothing is ever going to happen there." It would not be too much later that the Brian Nichols mass shooting at the Fulton County Courthouse would prove that theory to be false.

Even in the jail setting, officers need to be physically fit and able to defend themselves since they are outnumbered a hundred to one on every shift. But that was not the case at the Clayton County sheriff's office either at the time I was running. I wanted to reform this and that meant I had to make what leaders are supposed to make—a tough decision. I'm not going to act like I'm a football fan or knowledgeable about football, but I have friends who are and from listening to their conversations, here's the one thing I've learned: A football recruiter is looking for the most talented players he can get on his team. Many don't even get drafted. If members on the team are unproductive and they don't perform, they get cut from the team. In the world of sports, this is a very normal and common-sense thing, especially if someone is trying to win the Super Bowl. They simply need to have the fastest, strongest, and the brightest on the team. Well, if you use that analogy in the world of crime-fighting, common sense should dictate the philosophy should not be that much different. If I want to put people on the street that are expected to apprehend rapists, robbers, and murderers, they should be able to catch them if they take off running, be able to fight them and win if they start fighting and be able to handle themselves in a gunfight if they start shooting at them. They also need to have the reflex skills to handle a car if a dangerous suspect is fleeing from a serious crime in a motor vehicle. That is what the public expects us to be capable of doing to protect them.

But how can this happen if a sheriff hires or is forced to retain deputies who may get out of breath just from walking to the corner store? This is not to criticize people who are overweight and out of shape, but at no point do they go out for the NFL because they know they can't cut it. So why are they allowed to try out for a team where the skills of running, fighting, and driving are not only the skills needed to be successful with apprehending dangerous fugitives, but are the skills their lives and the lives of the public depend on? I need not add that if an NFL player became overweight and out of shape, he would logically be cut from the team. So, in a job where life and death are at stake instead of a trophy, why would making cuts not be reasonable?

If your job is to carry a gun to protect the citizens from those carrying guns to commit crimes against them, how can you do that if you're not proficient with the firearm you carry? When a person signs up for law enforcement, he's essentially saying he's willing to risk his life to get into a gunfight to protect the life of another person. The life that needs protection could very well be his own if he's ambushed. He knows, or at least should know, there's a possibility that if he's ever put in a situation where he's in a gunfight, it can well be with someone who is a well-trained gunfighter. But who should be more well-trained at gunfighting than law enforcement? If your child is in school and a deranged gunman walks in, wouldn't you like to know the people who are charged with rescuing them are well-trained and proficient with their firearms, capable of rescuing your child? Well, that can't be if they only must fire their weapons once a year and only are required to be 70 to 80 percent accurate.

I wanted to put together a team that could win the Super Bowl of crime fighting. If I was going to be effective at transforming the sheriff's office into a crime-fighting machine, I needed deputies capable of running after robbers to catch and tackle them, so they did not escape custody, just like tacklers in a football team have to be able to tackle the quarterback or wide receiver. I needed deputies capable of hostage rescues, which meant they had to be proficient with their firearms and hit the hostage taker instead of the hostage. If you saw what the Clayton County sheriff's office looked like in 2004, it was nowhere close to winning a flag football tournament with kindergartners. To have the team I envisioned, that I knew could reduce crime, I was going to have to make cuts to the team that was there.

Now, in the world of sports, this makes perfect sense. But because of the way the civil service system was set up for the sheriff's office in Clayton County, I was pretty much stuck with an administration mostly made up of the exact opposite of what was needed to get crime under control, and I was not sure how I would be able to bring in a new team to fulfill the vision. But an answer would come. After I ran and won the election, while waiting to take office, I continued to do as much research on the office of sheriff as I could. I got in touch with the director of the Georgia Sheriffs'

Association, and he provided me with a lot of case law that specified exactly where the office of sheriff authority lies.

While reading what was sent to me, I came across case law that could help me get to my goal of bringing in my own team. Some of the case law provided covered civil service, which the sheriff's office was under at the time. Civil service is a two-edged sword. It is designed to protect the jobs of government workers and give them a board to appeal their terminations or discipline to. Its purest intentions are not a bad thing, but again, all politics are local, so if an employee who has done something wrong has a friend on the civil service board, he can be pretty much guaranteed to get away with anything. The Civil Service Board went as far as to adjust the discipline given to sheriff's office employees. For example, if you suspended a person for five days, they would come back and drop it to one day or reverse it altogether, whether the employee committed the infraction or not. It was a system really meant for department heads, not elected officials who were tasked with picking their own department heads.

But in Clayton County, they decided to put the offices of elected officials under civil service, which gave a newly elected official very few options when he came to office as to who he could have on his staff. Imagine a race with a political opponent, and after you defeat him, you are now stuck with his whole administrative staff.

But, fortunately, the director of the sheriff's association was sending me copies of all the case law rulings that said for a sheriff's office employee to be under civil service, two things had to take place. Number one, the sheriff had to make a request to the board of commissioners to place his employees under civil service and, number two, the board of commissioners had to vote to do so. That ruling stated if one existed without the other, the employees were never legally placed under civil service.

Well, I did my research and confirmed neither of the two had occurred. No sheriff in the history of Clayton had ever requested the sheriff's office be under civil service and there was never a vote by the board of commissioners. The case law even went on to state that employees of the sheriff are not employees of the County but employees of the state. This is a very difficult concept for a lot of commissioners to comprehend because the board of commissioners fund the sheriff's office because they're required, by state law, to do so but that does not give them any other authority over the office of sheriff. This unique governmental structure is both a curse and a blessing at the same time. Because the board of commissioners are responsible for paying the sheriff's office bills by law, they feel they should have control over it despite the law giving the sheriff total autonomy. When this type of government was set up, I doubt anybody thought about human nature coming into play with this.

Once, I read this case that showed the Clayton County sheriff's office was not placed under civil service. I wanted to make sure I was interpreting what I was reading correctly, even though it was written very plainly. I consulted with two attorneys and had them read the case law to get their professional opinion of whether the employees at the sheriff's office were legally under civil service or not. Both, including one who was the lawyer for the Georgia Sheriffs' Association at that time, gave me the legal opinion they were not under civil service. Based on both of their opinions, I knew I was on good legal grounds to bring in my own administration. But there were many who did not agree with how I brought in the new administration. Even if I had done it in a different way, they would have fought against it. They just capitalized on *how* I did what I did, completely ignoring *why* I did what I did. But there was a very good reason for how I did it.

Chapter 5

Snipers on the Roof

I t has been said that war is politics with bloodshed, and politics is war without bloodshed. The 2000 Dekalb County sheriff's race proved that theory to be wrong. Metro Atlanta would soon find out the world of local politics *could* result in bloodshed as well.

I already knew I was going to run for sheriff in 2004 and was laying the groundwork to make it happen. So, in 2000, while watching the Clayton County sheriff's race, I was also watching the Dekalb County sheriff's race closely as well. There was a Dekalb County police captain named Derwin Brown who was running for sheriff. He caught my attention because he seemed to be interested in making the changes to the sheriff's office, I thought someone should have made years ago. He was running against the incumbent Sydney Dorsey, who was an ex-homicide detective in Atlanta who made a name for himself in the Wayne Williams, missing children case. Derwin Brown surprised everyone when he defeated Sid Dorsey. I was excited because I was looking forward to seeing exactly what type of changes he was going to make that I could perhaps implement in Clayton County. I thought he would be the trailblazer we needed to restore the metro office of sheriff back to what it was intended to do instead of making excuses and taking the second chair to county police who did not have the constitutional authority and jurisdiction needed to really get the job of fighting crime done.

I, nor the world, would ever get to see what he would've done, because we all were about to get robbed of Derwin Brown's life.

I remember waking up to a phone call, saying I needed to get up and cut my tv on because something had happened to the sheriff elect in Dekalb County. It turned out the incoming Sheriff Derwin Brown was assassinated in his front yard after coming back from a party, celebrating his graduation from the Sheriff's Academy. I was still a homicide detective at the time and my instincts based on training instantly told me it was someone within the sheriff's office that was the culprit of this murder. While at the Sheriff's Academy, Derwin Brown had sent out letters to thirty-seven employees, informing them their services would no longer be needed when he got into office. There was no doubt in my mind that somewhere within the scope of those thirty-seven letters would be the trigger man (or trigger men) responsible for this murder. Put a pin in this: the people who pose the greatest danger to any elected sheriff are not inmates or street thugs, it is the employees he must discipline or fire that are the sheriff's greatest danger. It was the employees Derwin fired who shot and killed him in his front yard. And as you will read, it was employees I fired and disciplined—with the help of the Clayton DA—that plotted to have me indicted.

Upon investigation, it was discovered that one of Derwin Brown's shooters was making a six-figure salary by having his overtime padded. Losing a six-figure salary of padded overtime gave him a vested interest in seeing to it that Derwin Brown did not make it to the office of sheriff. As you will read further, many of the witnesses against me at my trial were employees I had fired. Guess what for? Stealing $1.5 million in padded overtime. When the case was sent to the Clayton County DA's office, she did not prosecute them. I wonder why? Let me repeat: the most dangerous people for an elected sheriff are not the robbers and murderers in his jail or gangs on the street, but the disgruntled employees that have been disciplined, fired, or simply have their own agenda they can't get done with that person in power.

Now let's fast forward to 2004. I, along with the rest of the world, watched a man elected as sheriff get gunned down and killed in his front yard for trying to remove his predecessor's administration to bring in his own. I too was planning on bringing in my own administration and replacing the lackluster one within the Clayton County sheriff's office. Who is to say that what happened to Derwin Brown could not happen to me?

My race for sheriff caused a lot of tension in Clayton County. Once the campaign got started and the momentum began building, it became obvious the sheriff I was running against was in danger of being defeated. A lot of things began to occur that brought about the need for my security. The chief of police did a commercial with the sitting sheriff I was running against and had me transferred from the robbery-homicide division to the evidence room, stripping me of my assigned vehicle. Now, this is not a big deal, however, at the same time, another police officer working for Clayton County was also running for sheriff. He was *not* transferred and did *not* have his vehicle taken.

The Clayton County board of commissioners also got on the

bandwagon team to stop me from winning the sheriff's seat. The board of commissioners came up with an ordinance, saying that if anyone who worked for the county ran for office, they would have to take an unpaid leave of absence to run. This ordinance was created just for me because in the previous sheriff's race, a Clayton County police sergeant, named Carlton Woods, ran for sheriff against Stanley Tuggle in 2000 and was allowed to run free of any restrictions of absence without pay. There would be further proof this ordinance was designed to target me because in the 2012 race, when the commissioners wanted to support a female police candidate for sheriff, they voted to repeal the ordinance so she could run. Even though they got the ordinance passed, they could not enforce it on me because they were shown case law that their ordinance had not passed the preclearance required by the Justice Department for the ordinance to be enforced. This was just the beginning of many plots by political enemies to stop or disqualify me from the office of sheriff since they felt hopeless fighting me at the polls.

On election day, a friend of mine who had a security company came to pick me up with a few of his security guards. He thought it would be a good idea for me to have security that day considering what happened in Dekalb County and all the tension being created about me winning this race. As they escorted me into the back of the truck, I started hearing one of them shouting to someone, "What do you want?" and then I saw a silhouette run up to the truck, placing his face against the dark tinted windows. As one of them ordered him to get away from the truck, he took off running. When they got in, they told me the person was the Clayton County police officer who was also running for sheriff. Now, why would he be in front of my residence that early in the morning, waiting for me to come outside? I can only speculate, but I doubt it was to wish me good luck on winning the campaign.

On our way to the campaign headquarters, I called the police station to get an officer to meet me to write a police report about what occurred. Instead, they sent a police captain. When I told the captain what occurred and that I needed an incident report, he said no police report would be done because it was a political matter. When I asked him how, with what happened to Derwin Brown, someone running up to my vehicle identified as a police officer who was running against me—in the wee hours of the morning— a political matter? He got red in the face and stormed off because he could not answer the question.

I won my first bid for sheriff, defeating the incumbent and two other candidates, including the police officer who was stalking me at the front of my residence without a runoff. It was a sweet victory, but it was just the beginning of a political war that would span two decades.

Just like Derwin Brown wanted to remove his predecessor's cronies and bring in his own administration, I wanted to do the same but with a different ending. I knew there were at least twenty-seven employees I would no longer need who weren't going to perform to the level of standards I had planned for a transformation when I became sheriff. It is important that when the new administrator comes in, especially in this type of office, he's surrounded by people that he at least thinks he can trust until he finds out otherwise. But I was in a dilemma.

Derwin Brown sent separation letters in advance to people,

giving them a chance to prepare to find other employment. Brown must have been correct about the ones he did not need in his administration because in that list of people were the ones who pulled the trigger and ultimately assassinated him in his front yard. Knowing history has a nasty way of repeating itself, it made absolutely no sense for *me* to warn twenty-seven people ahead of time that they were no longer going to have their jobs. By this time, regular, unarmed employees in the civilian sector had already been well established for "going postal" at jobs where they were being dismissed or disciplined. Therefore, in undertaking the task of firing twenty-seven people who carry firearms, including fully automatic rifles depending on the assignment, as part of their jobs, common sense would dictate that extra security measures might be wise. Especially considering the sheriff in the neighboring county had been assassinated for the same thing.

As a result, I came up with a security plan to safely dismiss the twenty-seven people on my first day in office to prevent anyone who would be at the sheriff's office that day from getting hurt. The plan was simple: all the people who were going to be dismissed would be notified in an area where no one was allowed to carry firearms. They would then be dismissed out of the back sallyport area, where two of the people in my new administration would be on the roof, watching. Why? Because some of the twenty-seven people who were going to be dismissed had been assigned both marked and unmarked patrol cars—some of which held fully automatic rifles. We decided that, as a safety precaution, we would have two sharpshooters on the roof with access to their weapons in case they saw one of the fired deputies take hold of one of those weapons. There was a leak that some deputies were going to be fired so there were cameras already outside filming the two deputies on the roof. Contrary to what our local tabloid media reported, these two sharpshooters did not brandish or point any weapons at anyone. If they did, the local tabloid media would have produced a picture or footage to show it and those images would be available on Google today. There are none because it never happened.

Although the plan was simple common sense for the safety of all involved and not involved, by the end of the day, it became perhaps the most exploited terminations in the nation. All we needed was for local tabloid media to put their spin on it and spin it they did. They spun it as a black sheriff putting snipers on the roof, pointing rifles at employees being fired. Those two deputies did exactly what I ordered them to do, observe, and if they saw a situation turning violent, they had what they needed to stop people from getting hurt. They were ordered not to take any action unless I okayed it. But it would not stop there. Not only did the media say that people were fired with snipers pointing weapons at them (which never occurred), they made it appear as though I was an African American sheriff only firing deputies *because* they were white. I fired white and black. Race had nothing to do with who was fired, but corruption and nonperformance did. Most importantly, no one got hurt because preemptive measures were taken to make sure that did not occur.

That situation would carry on and on in the media and courts for most of the first three years of my first term in office. Fortunately, I caught on within the first year that explaining your actions to the media—no matter how logical it is—was and will always be a waste of time, so I began concentrating on what I came to the office to do; fight crime. I could have gotten it done much faster and smoother had I not been forced to keep the administration of my predecessor by an injunction, but I was determined to get the transformation done—and getting it done was what I did.

Chapter 6

"Sheriff on Deck"

N
ow I was in office, stuck with my predecessor's administration, which was very dysfunctional, to say the least.
It has been said that it is easier to run with one hundred
people who want to go with you rather than with one hanging
around your neck. That is why the first option, if available like the
NFL, is to cut the ones from your team that would be hanging
around your neck. But that option was not available, so I had to
find a way to fulfill the vision and get the mission done.

There is another leadership principle always present and necessary that I learned and learned fast, a principle that would allow
me to succeed and exceed expectations under those circumstances.
This principle is the exact opposite of the age-old adage, "You can lead
a horse to the water, but you can't make him drink." This is perhaps
the biggest excuse adage known to man that produces, maintains, and
keeps weak, ineffective leaders in leadership positions. Effective
leaders don't buy into this adage at all. If the horse does not drink
the water, real leaders pour the water down their throats. If that
does not work, they get an IV injection for the horse. No excuses
because if you accept that you can't make the horse drink, you are
setting the horse up to collapse on the journey across the desert and
the rider is going to die as well because of this lackadaisical excuse.

Does the horse like this? Of course not. No one likes anyone making them do their jobs to a higher level even if it leads to the promised land. But this type of leadership gets the results needed to get the mission done. This is what I had to do with the administration I was forced to keep who were fighting, kicking, and screaming the whole way. They did not like the type of police work I made them do, but what I made them do worked and kept the crime down. For example, I would require my deputies to sit in front of drug houses twenty-four hours a day so that drug dealers could not sell drugs and force them to leave the county. No one enjoyed this boring, monotonous duty, and they bitched and moaned over it every day. Some claimed that it was too dangerous, and others hinted unconstitutional.

However, open air drug trafficking was put under control for the first time in the county's history and the crime started going down. It worked.

The Clayton County Jail, at that time, was like most of the jails in the metro area. It was unsafe, nasty, smelled bad, and was way out of control. Under my predecessor, inmates had gotten a video camera into jail to show just how much fun they were having recording themselves smoking weed, drinking liquor, and indulging in other things that, logically, should not have been in the jail. My predecessor also had several escapes under his watch, including two murderers who, after escaping, got into a shootout with law enforcement out of state where they were captured. Add to this that a lot of inmates were killing themselves in jail by hanging themselves from their bunks. Some inmates would throw urine and feces on officers whenever they got mad or for no real reason at all;

and if you walked into certain areas like maximum security, inmates would yell and scream and beat the doors and windows so loud, officers could not hear themselves talk. It was a situation no one in the corrections business for years had found a way to control. My expertise was violent crime, not corrections, but I knew a jail could be better controlled. It was not years of jail experience that would be needed, just good old common sense.

The local county jail is the first defense or front line in crime fighting in any county. Show me the state of a county jail and I can show you the state of the county as far as crime is concerned. Here is why. We must always remember the jail is a microcosm of the streets surrounding it. The people who make up the criminal population in a county are in and out of their county jail. This gives the sheriff a unique opportunity to introduce himself to every criminal in his county because every criminal in the county is either currently staying with him at the jail or making frequent trips to the jail. Therefore, if the sheriff cannot control his own house in the county jail, how can he possibly control the streets?

A jail should be a controlled environment where the sheriff can control all ingress and outward movements. So, if he can't control the amount of drugs inside his jail, which should be zero, how can he possibly control drug trafficking on the streets? But let's take it a step even further. If the sheriff cannot control the violence in his jail, how can he control violence on the streets? I don't need to meet the sheriff to know what kind of sheriff he is, all I need to do is walk through his jail and it tells me everything I need to know. If a sheriff can't control his jail, I already know he can't control the streets because the jail is a controlled environment. I have seen jails I won't name where the inmates curse and make threats to the sheriff on the rare occasions he walks through. If criminals feel emboldened to treat the sheriff and his staff that way inside of jail, what happens if the sheriff runs into one of these criminals at a local supermarket?

The respect for the sheriff's office that is needed to maintain law and order on the streets begins at the county jail. If inmates feel comfortable throwing urine and feces on officers, masturbating in front of females, and attacking officers at will, knowing they have nothing to fear while they are in jail, they are even more emboldened once they're released on the street. If the protectors can't control the individuals, they are supposed to protect society from, then there truly is no protection for anyone. Jails must be a controlled environment for the safety of not just officers and the civilian staff working there, but also for the inmates who can fall prey to other inmates. I had to find a way to control violent inmates without using violence and find it, I did.

Even though my political enemies ultimately used my methodology against me—saying they were unconstitutional despite training and policy that supported my methods to put me in the prison I am in while writing this book—these tactics were not only effective, safe, and lawful, they actually worked, making my jail the safest and cleanest jail in the state of Georgia, minimizing injuries to officers and inmates. The following are the methods and tools I used to control the Clayton County Jail to make it safe for all who worked there as well as the inmates who stayed there.

Please note that since my indictment, these methods are *not* currently being used out of fear of politically motivated prosecution initiated by the Clayton County DA. As a result, the Clayton County Jail has now become a dangerous place to work or be an inmate. As I write this book, four inmates have been murdered and one was accidently killed by officers who were trying to stop him from killing himself but were too afraid to use the safety restraint chair. This is the result of what happens when prosecutors are allowed to make up crimes to prosecute law enforcement for politically motivated purposes, leaving officers afraid to use the few tools they have left to prevent and control potentially violent inmates.

Contraband and Weapons

The basic ingredient to controlling a jail is very simple. You simply have to take control of what goes in and out of the jail. Most jails have multiple ways to get in and out, and in the majority of our nation's jails, the officers, as well as the civilians who work there, can come in and out of the jail, unchecked. If no one's checking those who enter the multiple ways to get into the jail, then *anything* can enter the jail—from drugs to weapons to firearms, which occurred at the Fulton County Jail in Atlanta years ago, where an inmate shot another inmate over a drug deal.

At the Clayton County Jail, I closed all entrances to the jail except one for all employees, including civilian and sworn officers. Everyone entering the jail, regardless of rank or position, had to be searched—including me. If an employee left the jail just for five minutes to take a smoke or go to his car, upon returning, that employee would have to be searched again. A camera was placed to record the search of employees, to make sure it was being done thoroughly and that those charged with searching knew their search was being recorded. I also had access to this video camera to watch live from my phone, to make sure they were searching employees to my specifications. Every now and then, at random, a drug dog would be placed at this entrance to detect the odor of any type of drug while employees were coming in and being searched. Just doing this kept the jail free from contraband and drugs. I did not fully appreciate how effective this was and the far-reaching effects until one day, I got contacted by an inmate who said he wanted to thank me for getting him off drugs. When I asked him how I was the one who got him off drugs, he told me the Clayton County Jail was the only jail he'd ever been in where he did not have access to drugs. He said as a result, he was able to detox himself cold turkey and never returned to taking them again.

"The Hill-ton": Georgia's Toughest Paramilitary Jail

Every organization has a culture, and that culture must be set by the leader. No one else can set a culture except the leader, because everything must start from the top down. My vision was to turn the Clayton County Jail into a paramilitary jail to resemble the atmosphere of a military boot camp. There is a culture in jails of chaos and dysfunction which leads to riots, escapes, inmate-on-inmate violence, as well as inmate-on-officers violence. When you set a paramilitary culture just in discipline alone, the problems of disorderly conduct and chaos begin to cease. It was probably the best thing we could have ever done because most of the young men who came to jail never went to the military and unfortunately would never get the opportunity to go because of the crimes they were committing. In foreign countries I have visited where every eighteen-year-old is required to serve in the military, the discipline of the country overall is better, and the crime rate is lower. There was a time in the past when judges would sentence young men giving them the option to serve that time by enlisting in the military. How or why, that stopped, I do not know, but that is probably one of the biggest mistakes that was ever made.

It was amazing to see how the young men who came to the Clayton County Jail responded to the military discipline. When the public would come and take tours, they were amazed to see how clean the jail was and how they kept their beds made.

Inmates had to go to attention when a commanding officer was on deck, address the staff as sir or ma'am, and keep their areas clean to military standards. There was one variation and that was to have inmates face the wall when going to attention. There are two main reasons inmates had to face away when staff walked by. The first reason is safety and security because it's difficult to attack someone you can't see. This almost completely stopped the sexual harassment from inmates to females. This also prevented the inmates from staring others down in a threatening manner.

When inmates face the wall, they also had to have their hands behind their back so we could see exactly what was in their hands. This was in line with basic officer safety training because all law enforcement officers are trained from day one to watch the hands—because hands kill.

Disciplinary Lock Down

Disciplinary lockdown is a very effective method when dealing with controlling potential riot-type incidents in the jail. It is also a powerful deterrent for any future crazy behavior. When inmates are involved in behaviors that give them access to contraband and gathering for gang-like riot behavior, lockdown is needed. During lockdown, all privileges such as phone, commissary, and recreation are suspended. If a housing unit becomes disruptive, it only takes two to three days of disciplinary lockdown, and 95 percent of them will become and remain compliant. The "elite" 5 percent who remain disruptive are usually the candidates for maximum security.

Most sheriffs have absolutely no control over maximum security because inmates in maximum security have already lost every privilege, so they feel they have nothing to lose or fear—just as kids now do in public schools since they removed corporal punishment. The first time I walked into the maximum-security unit, I could not hear myself talk over the yelling, banging, and kicking of the jail cell doors. Inmates were beating the doors with their fists and kicking them with their feet while yelling profanities. Anytime officers had to go in for cell checks, they were in danger of having urine or feces thrown on them. Nobody had a solution on how to control inmates in this section. But there was a very effective and nonviolent way to bring peace to the valley, that was the introduction of Nutraloaf to the Clayton County Jail.

Nutraloaf

Nutraloaf is the unofficial name for special meal management. Nutraloaf is a loaf of an assortment of very nutritious ingredients, it is not a loaf of bread. Some of the ingredients include oatmeal, corn, and greens, to name a few, that provide nutrients to the body. By law, the sheriff must provide a nutritious meal, not a gourmet meal. I have eaten Nutraloaf myself. Nutraloaf is not bad, but it is not a five-star experience either. It is very bland and does not leave you with the satisfaction you get after eating at your grandmother's house. However, it is very nutritious.

Nutraloaf cured the problems we were having in maximum security and cured most of the other problems we had with unruly and violent inmates. After I signed off on the policy and gave the go to Nutraloaf, I walked down to maximum security and stood there for fifteen minutes while inmates continued to beat on the walls, yelling and screaming profanities. Afterward, I left and gave the word to prescribe three days of Nutraloaf for everyone.

Not everyone in maximum security was placed on Nutraloaf. The policy for Nutraloaf stated that everyone had to be medically cleared before they could be given the special meal management. Medical doctors had to make sure there weren't any diabetics or anyone who had any type of condition that could be adversely affected by Nutraloaf. Also, everyone had to be weighed every day to make sure there was no rapid weight loss that would cause any measure of concern.

So, except for maybe two or three inmates who were not medically cleared, everyone else in maximum security was put on Nutraloaf. Everyone was told I would be back in three days and then if I heard a pin drop, they would remain on it for an additional three days. When I returned, not only could I not hear a pin drop, but the inmates were also paramilitary-ready, going to attention without fail. From that moment on, we regained and maintained control of maximum security. As a matter of fact, when my dearly departed ninety-year-old (at the time) grandmother came to visit me, I walked her through the entire jail and, yes, through maximum security. Not one cursed a word, no screaming, no banging on the doors, only responses to paramilitary commands. My grandmother was very impressed.

Nutraloaf was very effective but was still merely a response *after* the action of an inmate. It did act as a deterrent to future actions, but it did not prevent the inmates from committing the first act. If the first act is just theft or the destruction of property, it is no big deal. But if the first act is an act of violence to another inmate or officer, anything done after the fact does very little to help the victim. It has been said a wise general foresees problems and prevents them before they occur. I've always been adamant about preventing things before they occur. The only way to reduce the murder rate is to stop people having the ability to murder. I would rather reduce the murder rate by 25 percent than say we have increased the solvability rate of murders by 25 percent. If we prevent murders, people don't die. If we solve the murders, we can't resurrect those who are dead.

But how can you prevent ambushes and acts of violence in jail before they occur? The answer is not that complicated. All peace officers are trained in how to use restraints as a preventative control measure. It's just that most don't use the option provided by training and case law. I always have employed this training as far back as when I was a rookie cop, and I credit it a lot to being alive and uninjured after thirty years in law enforcement. There is a tool that helped us accomplish this objective in jail, and that tool is the safety restraint chair.

Safety Restraint Chair

Safety restraint chairs are not just used in jails. They are also used in schools and hospitals. There have been some lawsuits over its use in schools where some disagreed about when and how it should be used, but interestingly no one was sent to federal prison because of it until now—and I am the first in history.

Simply putting a violent inmate on disciplinary lockdown is not only ineffective, but unsafe. If the inmate is violent and simply put in a disciplinary lockdown, you stand the risk of officers being assaulted when they do their cell checks. You also stand the risk that if he's violent against himself, he has the freedom to do things that could cause self-harm—even if it's just banging his head or arms against a steel door.

A violent inmate is also able to take his violence out by destroying government property or converting objects into weapons to use against other inmates or officers. When an inmate is in a violent state of mind and the officer—based on his prior knowledge and experience from training and policy—can see this, the safety restraint chair is the safest and most humane way to prevent them from carrying out acts of violence. It also has a calming effect to deter future violence because it was rare those who were restrained acted out violently again.

There is statistical data at the Clayton County Jail that using the safety restraint chair for inmates who showed pre-attack indicators prevented violence in the jail. After its use was suspended because of my politically motivated prosecution, assaults on officers went up over 150 percent, and inmate-on-inmate assaults went up over 200 percent. Also as mentioned, after the restraint chair use was suspended, four inmates have been murdered in the jail and one was accidently killed by officers trying to restrain a suicidal inmate by keeping him pinned to the ground instead of restraining him in a safety restraint chair. No murders happened under my watch when we used the preventative method of using the safety restraint chair pre-emptively.

I will always recommend its use because it was and still is the safest and most humane way to prevent violence in jail. Political enemies using the safety restraint chair to wrongfully convict me to get me out of office because they could not beat me at the polls, cannot change the fact that the safety restraint chair worked and kept the jail safe. What they did just to put me here and get me out of the way has resulted in four inmates being murdered, numerous inmates being stabbed, as well as employees being injured. My use of the safety restraint chair protected officers from sudden attacks by inmates, inmates from attacking other inmates, and inmates from harming themselves and destroying property.

Because of these preventive, nonviolent tactics, such as the use of the safety restraint chair, military discipline, and Nutraloaf, the Clayton County Jail became the cleanest and safest jail in the state of Georgia and perhaps in the world. There were no escapes, riots, or murders under our administration, and we were able to cut the suicides down to a rare event. This was a huge accomplishment for my first term, and I remain thankful to the team that helped achieve this milestone in jail management.

Fighting Crime

While restoring law and order to the Clayton County Jail, we were also working simultaneously to restore law and order to the streets of Clayton County. We began to make our mark with pro-active policing that was just as effective as what we were doing in the jail. Even though what we were doing to clean up the streets was working and getting results, there was constant criticism and interruptions from political enemies and the media. This, of course, is normal. I think we all know now that if someone could figure out how to heal the sick and raise the dead, there would be someone out there saying that it was not FDA-approved and complaining about how bringing back the dead is a liability because of potential overcrowding. There is, and will always be an antagonist, especially if that person feels what you do could possibly rain on a parade they were planning.

Our main antagonist of course was Jeff Turner. Not too long after I won the election for sheriff, the county commission appointed Jeff Turner, who is now the sitting chairman of the board of commissioners, as the new police chief. I knew this was going to be a disaster for the county as far as tackling crime because all of the years I had worked with Turner when I was a county policeman and a homicide detective, I saw firsthand how weak he was as a cop from my first week on the job and later as a supervisor who sued to get promoted. I knew he would be the same as a police chief. Even to this day, in his role as the chairman of the county, he remains pusillanimous, and the county is suffering as a result.

As time went on, and we began achieving results in the art of crime fighting, Turner became very bitter about what the sheriff's office was doing. Not because it wasn't effective, but because it was raining on his parade and making the police under his leadership look ineffective. We were not trying to make them look ineffective. They were just ineffective. Turner constantly ran to local media to complain about me "doing his job" every chance he got, and it seemed as if he forgot more and more what his actual job was, while focusing on how I should do my job. He was very angry about the sheriff's office doing police work and he became obsessed with stopping us from fighting crime instead of joining us in fighting crime.

It didn't matter what it was or how effective it was, it was always a problem for Turner. For instance, when we created the Stalking unit to deal with domestic violence by "stalking the stalkers" instead of waiting for them to assault or kill women, Jeff Turner made a comment to local media that it was just a way of harassing men.

Turner even went as far as to blame my deputies for an armed robber who escaped from his officers who allegedly had the robber in a store, surrounded. Turner said if my deputies had not responded with lights and sirens, the robber would not have run out of the back door and escaped from them. I asked Turner if his officers had the store surrounded, why weren't they covering the back when the robber ran out and escaped? Turner did not have an answer for this and got wide-eyed like a deer in the headlights and stormed off.

Regardless of the constant distraction of Chief Turner and the media, the sheriff's office continued to move full force ahead and it is a good thing we did because nothing would have gotten done otherwise. We had an impact on crime that was felt in the streets and that needed to happen regardless. In the first term of my administration, in 2006, we successfully cleared the top ten most wanted fugitives list. We closed the infamous Poker Palace, which was allowed to go untouched even though the police department had information not only about gambling but drug trafficking as well. The owner of the Poker Palace attempted to bribe me for protection after he saw me raiding every illegal establishment in the county. When my VICE unit shut down his establishment, he and another person involved in the attempt to bribe me were charged with bribery as well. A local magistrate judge was inside the Poker Palace gambling when we shut it down and was locked up in a raid as well. That did not win me any new friends in the judicial community.

But there was another, bigger criminal enterprise that needed to be dealt with that made my relationship with the police chief even more contentious. There were thirteen massage parlors in Clayton County for as long as I can remember. Every now and then, Clayton County Police would send undercover people into the massage parlor to make an arrest. They would only arrest the girl soliciting the undercover officer and take her to jail while leaving the massage parlor open to continue business as soon as they walked out of the door. But the real problem with the massage parlors was probably far deeper than just prostitution. Undercover agents that went into massage parlors found out most of the girls were under sexual servitude imported from foreign countries against their will to be pimped. This information was out there for quite a while but no one at the Clayton County Police or DA's office wanted to address it. I often still wonder, why?

I gave my VICE unit the assignment to go in and shut all of them down once and for all and free all the girls being held against their will. Somehow, Turner got word we were working the massage parlor houses and he did not want to get shown up again for doing nothing so he decided to do a sting operation, called his friends in the media, and had them cover the story when he raided one massage parlor. He made a big media production out of it by walking into the massage parlor after the raid. What was sad was they, as usual, only arrested two or three girls who performed the act with the undercover cops and left with them while the parlor remained open for business and the other girls continued to be kept captive and forced to perform sexual acts. What Turner missed was that we were not doing a sting to arrest a few girls for a quick news story, but we were going to shut the entire operation down so we could free the women being used as sex slaves against their will.

It took a few months to get all the information needed under the RICO statute, but we finally had what we needed to get this operation done. When we went to the chief magistrate court judge, my VICE unit tried to obtain search warrants for all thirteen locations, but she only agreed to give them seven. The chief magistrate said she felt what we were doing was political and would not give Turner a chance to hit the massage parlors as well. The guys in my unit were flabbergasted because they'd never heard of such a thing from a judge. Fortunately, my commander had enough good sense to go to another judge and explain the severity of the situation about girls being held against their will. That judge immediately signed the search warrants for the other establishments.

Ironically, the day we hit all the massage parlors and shut them down, fell on the Emancipation Proclamation Day, the day when

African Americans were set free as slaves. That was not planned, it just happened.

When we shut the massage parlors down, we had already planned to have US Immigrations on hand for all the girls being held against their will. We did not arrest them, we freed them so they could be sent back to their countries free from sexual servitude. It was a great feeling to free these girls from what they'd been subjected to for years because of the politics and lackadaisical law enforcement in Clayton County that turned a blind eye to what was happening to them. Once this happened, the massage parlors never reopened again in "my county."

Fast forward to March 16, 2021, when the active shooter who shot up massage parlors in Atlanta was still at large. The Atlanta police chief called me to give me a heads up, suggesting I warn the massage parlors in my county to lock up and be careful. I told the police chief I appreciated it, but I closed all the massage parlors in "my county" in my first term, so there were none there for the guy to shoot up. There was a moment of silence on the phone followed by a "wow" and a chuckle.

It was at that moment I realized what an amazing job my VICE unit had done and wondered what became of all those young girls we freed. When anyone asks me what the most significant thing my administration accomplished in my first term, my answer will always remain that we helped free slaves on the day the Emancipation Proclamation was signed.

Chapter 7

Bring back the Crime Fighter

I n 2008, when I was up for reelection, I was not the least worried because we had done the job and I kept a close connection with the people. However, as good as I was at grassroots politics and policing, I still was not a trained political strategist. At least not yet. In this election cycle, three lawyers ran as a political slate. A former juvenile court judge, Tracy Graham Lawson, ran for district attorney; Tasha Mosley, a former assistant in the solicitor's office, ran for solicitor general; and Kem Kimbrough, a former legal advisor at the sheriff's office, ran against me for sheriff. All three of these lawyers were friends with each other and with my sworn public enemy, Police Chief Jeff Turner. All four of these individuals would become long-term political enemies.

These three attorneys hired a well-known local political strategist to help them with their campaigns. This move became the catalyst for me to not only hire one for all my future campaigns, but to train and learn to become one myself.

Losing Reelection

All of the polls showed I had more than 50 percent of the votes, so I was set to win reelection without a runoff. No one questioned that the streets and jail were under control. It was just all of the people I fired and their support group who were dead-set against me being reelected. The people I fired were hoping to get their jobs back under a new sheriff. None of this caused me any real concern as this type of politics is common in a sheriff's races.

There was one significant factor that had changed the landscape of the electorate that overwhelmingly elected me in 2004. Many citizens who supported me as the sheriff moved to neighboring counties because of a fiasco that happened with the school board losing its accreditation. Even though a large percentage of my base had left, I was still favored to win 51 percent of the vote. But 51 percent is a thin margin to poll at and anything can flip that type of thin margin.

On the night of the election, as the numbers came in, it clearly showed me winning over 50 percent until the final numbers from the last precinct came in and brought me under the 50 percentiles mark I needed to win without a runoff. In most states, whoever gets most of the votes wins. But in Georgia, they still do runoffs, which means if more than one person runs against you, you must get 50 percent of the votes plus one to win outright. If no one does this, the two candidates with the most votes must face off again at the polls about a month later. When Kimbrough and I went to the runoff election, the numbers married the same thing that happened during the primary. All the precincts came back showing I had won over 50 percent, but when the final precinct came in, which was the early and absentee votes, it brought me right under the 50-percentile mark needed to win the election. Kimbrough and the other two attorneys who ran as a slate with him had won the election. But how?

It was too late, but I still hired a political analyzer to study the race to see how and why I lost. After their analysis, I had to salute the strategist my political enemies hired. It turns out, they used a crossover strategy. Clayton County is the most Democratic County in the state of Georgia. This means whoever wins the Democratic primary has won the election because there are not enough Republican votes in the county to win a general election in November, which coincides with the presidential race. This strategist solicited several Republican voters in the county to cross over in the Democratic primary to help the political slate, which helped my opponent barely make it over the 50 percent threshold to beat me at the polls. It was a hard and costly lesson to learn. But once I learned, I knew I would never let it happen again. I also knew that when I ran again, I would win if I could counter that strategy. I would then set out on a quest to find the best political consultants in the business, not just to run my future campaign, but to train me so I could run my own and anyone else's campaign I desired.

Unfortunately for Clayton County, in addition to having a weak and ineffective police chief, they now had an even weaker leader as sheriff. I didn't have to sit and wait to see if the crime would go up with Kem Kimbrough as sheriff and Turner as chief. I *knew* crime would go up. Clayton County is not the type of county that a Barney Fife-type sheriff or Andy Griffin-type chief can control due to the level of thugs we have in the county. I also knew Jeff Turner wouldn't last long as the police chief. He really became chief on a fluke of being in the right place at the right time after suing the county over the years to get promoted when he could not pass the promotional exam. Unfortunately, the board of commissioners did not know where or how to look for a real chief, so they just went with him. It was barely over a year after I lost reelection that the board of commissioners got rid of Jeff Turner due to his lackluster performance. Turner's replacement was Greg Porter, who was once his best friend. Turner had promoted him to deputy chief out of friendship. Both had convinced the previous chief to send them to Command College and the FBI academy, but neither showed the ability to command a playground fight or find a prostitute in a prostitution house. When Porter took over, he and Kimbrough began to feud as well. As I predicted, crime went back up and the jail went back out of control.

Incidents began to occur in the county that made it obvious Kimbrough and Porter had lost control. The same bank got robbed twice in twenty-four hours. Police officers' cars were being broken into regularly and some had automatic weapons being stolen from them that belonged to SWAT team members. One night, bandits stole a marked police car and took it for a joy ride. They dumped the car in a ditch on the side of the road, took all the officer's belongings, and threw them on the ground. From these actions, it was obvious the fear and respect for law enforcement in Clayton County was gone. My distractors have always criticized me for putting fear in criminals. But for this, I will never apologize because the lawlessness I am describing that took place after my departure only occurs when criminals know they have nothing or no one to fear. If you live in a county where criminals don't fear acting out because of who the sheriff is, it means it's time to find a new sheriff.

These truths, along with another one of my predictions, came true in the worst way. One day, I stopped at a QT Store on Riverdale Road to get gas. I was amazed at the number of thugs that were hanging out on the north side of the store. When I was in office, one of the main things we did was stop loitering in front of stores because it breeds dangerous situations, as we saw in a neighboring county where a young lady was killed by thugs that were loitering in front of a store. One of the thugs I observed caught my attention because he appeared to be leading the crowd. He was an Asian male who was bebopping hard to some hip-hop music.

Later that day, I was talking to a friend of mine on the Clayton County Police Force and I told him I had a bad feeling someone in law enforcement in the county was about to get killed. When he asked why, I explained to him that based on the type of instances occurring in the county—such as targeting law enforcement cars and weapons, and criminals being bold enough to rob the same bank twice in twenty-four hours—there was a lack of respect and fear for law enforcement that usually results in a deputy or officer being seriously injured or killed. I also told him I was disturbed about the number of thugs allowed to hang out in front of stores without being checked.

Two weeks later, a deputy was shot and killed at a traffic stop. The deputy was shot and killed by an Asian male who, when I saw the picture of him on TV, I instantly recognized as the Asian male hanging out with the other thugs in front of the QT on

Riverdale Road. He had an outstanding warrant for him for armed robbery. Proactive police work could have prevented this because if officers and deputies had checked all those loitering at the store that day with aggressive street sweeps, he would have already been taken into custody.

After I made my announcement that I was going to seek reelection for sheriff, Jeff Turner, the fired police chief, shortly thereafter made the announcement that he was going to run for sheriff too. Turner sent me a message through a mutual acquaintance that he was going to show me who was more popular. I sent him a message back, reminding him that he already told reporters he had only moved back to the county a year ago, and that the law said you needed to be in the county two years to run for sheriff. Turner backed out and bitterly ran for chairman instead, a job he never truly wanted, and it showed with his lackluster performance. As the election drew near, the chaos in the jail and on the streets continued and became the message for my campaign for reelection. The theme of the campaign was, "Bring Back the Crime Fighter." We filmed two political commercials. One commercial depicted criminals sitting around a table, talking about how well their criminal enterprise was going now that they had a weak sheriff. Then, one of the criminals got a phone call saying Sheriff Victor Hill was coming back and all the criminals started packing up to leave. The commercial ended with the statement, "Make criminals leave Clayton County. Bring back the crime fighter. Reelect Victor Hill for sheriff." The other had a "We need Batman to return" type of theme. It depicted the mayor being asked to bring me back because of the out-of-control crime by the city manager and putting out a bat light symbol with my badge and name across the sky. It had a comical punch line striking at the weakness of the new sheriff and got the message across. This message resonated with the voters, and it was clear I was the front-runner. My political opponent and his allies knew they were in trouble and had to do something, and do it fast, and do something they did. A ham sandwich indictment.

Thirty-Seven Count RICO Indictment

A couple of months after it was highly publicized, I would be seeking reelection for sheriff, the Clayton County DA, Tracy Graham Lawson, made an announcement she was assembling a special purpose grand jury to investigate corruption when I was sheriff. The timing was obvious to all. At this time, I had already been out of office for almost four years, so if there was corruption during my tenure, why wait to investigate three years later? Here is another reason why it was obvious the prosecution was politically motivated.

When Kim Kimbrough first got elected, he ordered a full-fledged investigation to see if they could find anything corrupt, which I had done while I was in office so he could come after me. After the investigation was concluded, the investigator admitted in his report he could not find any form of corruption that happened while I was in office. This proved they had no actual crime but were looking for one. I requested a copy of that investigation by means of the Open Records Act and made sure to send it to the district attorney's office so they could give it to their special purpose grand jury. This did not matter because they were not on a fact-finding mission, they were on a mission to create something that wasn't there.

Things started getting even more bizarre from this point. After being a detective for over a decade, I was well trained on how to follow (tail) someone. So, when I started *being* followed by sheriff's deputies, it was easy for me to detect it. Once you know someone is following you, unless they are very skilled, it's easy to trip them up. All you really have to do is go down a road you know is a dead end or circle the same block three or four times. If the same car is still with you, you are being followed. But who do you tell if the sheriff's office is following you? The sheriff's office is the highest law enforcement agency in the land, and the sheriff answers to only the people. Usually, when you tell people you're being followed, they think you're being paranoid, so I just continued to watch and have fun, losing my tails every day. I would later find out from sources present at a meeting that former Sheriff Kimbrough called in deputies and told them that their full-time job was to find anything they could on me. The source said Kimbrough told the deputies they did not have to come in and do anything else, just find something on Victor Hill.

We must ask though, if this was all about me being corrupt while I was in office, why were they following me three years later to see what I was doing rather than looking into what happened while I was in office? I still was not concerned about the special purpose grand jury because I knew I had not committed any crimes while I was in or out of office. I simply saw this as a sign Kimbrough, Lawson, and Tasha Mosley knew I was going to win and had become desperate. I figured they were just convening a special purpose grand jury to put my campaign under a "dark cloud" to try and suppress the amount of votes polling showed I would have. That theory would prove to be wrong.

The next thing they did had the special purpose grand jury indict a former employee of mine, Jonathan Newton. He held the position of Public Information Officer for a short while during my first term. Newton resigned after he was investigated for taking kickbacks from a printing company. For some reason, prosecutors did not want to prosecute him for this crime at the time, but now, suddenly, they were interested in charging him for something my office tried to have him arrested for during my first term in office three years prior. It turned out, as I would see from discovery evidence containing his video interview, the reason they charged him was that they were hoping I received some of the kickbacks he stole. Newton admitted during the interview that I had nothing to do with it and asked them for a deal admitting he was a thief. They later had to reindict Newton with another grand jury because Tracy Graham Lawson, Tasha Mosley, and Kem Kimbrough—all seasoned attorneys did not realize a special purpose grand jury could only *investigate*, not *indict*. This was their first political plot and it showed.

Around this time, I received a call from a local attorney, Steve Frey, who asked me if I thought I might need his help. I told him I appreciated the call and offer for help, but I had not committed any crimes I could be indicted for. Frey said, "Okay, well call me if you need me, because if they're going this far, they're looking to do something."

I replied, "What can they do if I haven't committed a crime?"

Frey then said something I will never forget. "Trust me when I tell you if they want to, they can indict anyone for anything, even if it's a ham sandwich." Steve knew what he was talking about. I have always heard the cliché: a DA can indict a ham sandwich. I thought it was more of a joke in the legal community, but I was getting ready to find out it was not a joke at all.

One evening, I got a knock at my door. There was an investigator from the DA's office named Dennis Baker, who was personal friends with a lot of the people I fired during my first term in office. He had been with the DA's office before I joined the Clayton County Police Department in 1992. His appearance, look, and demeanor could put you in the mind of one of the characters in the movie *Deliverance*. You could tell at a glance he probably never won a playground fight and had his lunch taken from elementary school until he got chased out of the high school door. Baker handed me a subpoena to appear before the grand jury with a proposed indictment. I called Steve Frey and hired him so he could be there to represent me before the grand jury. Another attorney and good friend, Musa Ghanayem, came to be there as well.

Before we went in front of the grand jury, Steve Frey called me and said something I'll never forget. "You do realize they are trying to indict you for stealing your assigned patrol car five times." I asked him if he was serious, and he said yes. He went on to say, "Twenty-seven of your charges are that you stole the same car five times. As a matter of fact, they are accusing you of stealing the same car three times in two weeks." He went on to say they charged me with a felony count for every time I put gas in the car and put this under the RICO Act saying, that by doing this, I was running a criminal enterprise.

I again said, "You've got to be kidding me."

He said, "No, I'm not." Frey reminded me of the phone call we had when he told me a DA can indict anyone for anything. He was right.

A DA and her investigators can go in and tell the grand jury anything they want to just to get the indictment to go through.

The grand jury will believe them because there is no way a prosecutor would lie to them, right? Unfortunately, many prosecutors lie just to get their target indicted. They pretty much know most people, when indicted, are shocked, scared, and don't have the money or the resources to fight back so it forces them to take a plea. But they were in for a surprise and a long ride with me because nothing would deter me from running, and I always fight back.

Indictment Day

On the day I went before the grand jury, the DA made a grand production of it in the media, and they were all waiting for me outside of the courthouse, along with some of the deputies that were surveilling me from on top of the courthouse. This was interesting since they were so critical of me having deputies on the roof when I fired the twenty-seven deputies in my first term in office.

The investigator who presented the case to the grand jury was a deputy I fired during my first term in office. The Clayton County DA got the grand jury to indict me, but only got it by one vote. Even some of the grand jury members figured out early that something did not seem right.

After it came back that I was indicted, I immediately went before a superior court judge for a bond hearing before being taken into custody. The judge set my bond for $50,000. The courtroom is connected to the jail in Clayton County so that when a person is taken into custody, there is a door from every courtroom that leads directly into the jail. After the judge set the bond, I began walking to the door leading to the jail where the court deputy was standing. The deputy steered me the other way. I was confused because there really was no other way to get to the jail other than to walk down the public hall and go way around the inside of the courthouse. I realized then that Kimbrough and the Clayton County DA had set up what we called a "perp walk." A "perp walk" is where you coordinate a walk in an area where the media is waiting. It is done for two reasons: to either embarrass the person arrested or to get the prosecutors and cops a chance to be on TV. Usually, it's both. The press was ready and waiting, and walked with me all the way down the hall as I was being escorted to jail. When a reporter asked me if there was anything I wanted to say, I said, "I'm still running for sheriff." That was not a bluff. I was and I intended on winning.

Once I arrived at the jail, I had enough money and people ready to bond me out instantly, but that would not be the case. It turned out, Kimbrough had threatened all the bonding companies that if they bonded me out, they could lose their ability to write bonds in Clayton County. He was hoping to keep me in custody long enough for the election to be over so I would not get a chance to put my name on the ballot. As a result, I ended up staying in jail for three days when I could have really been out in three hours.

My attorney brought the media down to do an interview. This was right before I cut off the media completely. It was an interesting interview. I made sure I sent Kimbrough and his allies, Tracy Graham Lawson and Tasha Mosley, a message: "It doesn't matter how long you keep me here. I'm only going to use it for rest because when I get out, I'm going to campaign, day and night, to make sure I win the election."

Winning Under Indictment

Once I was released from jail, I had one single goal in life—to beat Kimbrough and his political allies at the polls.

When I got out, I stayed true to my word, and I campaigned day and night and took the message to the people about bringing back the crime fighter. I did two political debates with Kem Kimbrough and ripped him a new butthole in each one. In one debate, when addressing how high the crime had gotten under his weak, Barney Fife leadership, I told him that deep down inside he wanted to vote for me too because he would feel safer with the protection I would provide for him, and his family. He didn't have a comeback for that because he knew it was the truth.

When election night came and the number of votes came back—in the words of the greatest boxer of all times—"I shocked the world" and beat the incumbent while under indictment. Kem Kimbrough, Tracy Graham Lawson, and DA Tasha Mosley were incensed—and so was the media.

Legal Eagle

So now, the DA and the media are mad because they can't believe their plan of indicting me and playing stories about the RICO indictment like I was a mob boss did not deter the voters from voting me back in office. They were also angry they could not scare me into taking a plea deal and bowing out. They tried to get the Governor to stop me from taking office, but Governor Deal had balls, seeing through the shenanigans. He decided to stay out of the fray and let it play out.

As we began to prepare for trial, it got more interesting once the discovery of evidence the state had to give us was provided, showing all of the evidence they allegedly had against me. Whoever gathered all the documents just happened to throw into the surveillance logs of seventeen deputies following me around for months. Remember when I said I was being followed? Now here was the proof I was not a conspiracy theorist. Let's think about this for a second. I'd already been out of office three years and allegedly this investigation was for what I did while I was in office. So, if that's the case, why are deputies following me around in 2012, documenting everywhere I go and taking photographs of me campaigning? That alone was proof this indictment was politically motivated. The media was aware of all of this. How do I know? Because I had someone send it to them. Not one time did they make a report on any of this. The only thing they would report consistently was that I was under a RICO indictment, making it look like I was some type of mob figure. Once my attorneys added up the total cost of my driving out of town and putting gas in my assigned police car, it came up to less than $2,000. There was a very legitimate reason why I was always in my assigned vehicle. It was because I was on call 24/7 and may have had to respond at any time of the day or night, especially if a deputy killed someone or got killed. By being in my assigned car, I could respond from wherever I was at. Even if I was not in my assigned car and had to get back, I had a credit card that I was authorized to use to purchase an emergency flight to get back to the county. That's a whole lot more expensive than just driving back in my assigned car.

Interestingly, history will show that the thirty-seven-count indictment was the largest RICO acquittal in Georgia, but the media failed to say it was about $2,000 of gas being put in a car, giving the impression I was running a criminal enterprise. But if you look at the amount of money spent having deputies follow me after I was out of office three years to conduct a corruption investigation while in office, it came up to about $400,000. No wonder crime was going up. The sitting sheriff made me number one on his top-ten most wanted while the real gangsters were having a field day raping, robbing, and murdering in Clayton County.

My attorney, Steve Frey, said that out of all the charges they stacked on me, only one of the charges made any sense, even though it was not a crime and very explainable. It turns out that when I took a trip out of town, I placed a hold with my county card instead of my actual card to hold the room for a personal vacation. That was easy to do because both the county card and my personal debit card were both visas. When I arrived at the location, I paid for the room with cash out of my own pocket, which obviously shows I had no intent to use county funds to pay for a hotel. It was hard to believe they wanted to go to trial on this, but they were too far in, and this was their only hope to get me out of office now that I had won the election.

RICO Trial

During the trial, my attorneys made the DA look like a jackass. They made it very clear to the jury that the only thing I was guilty of was running for sheriff. They dissected the stupidity of the case. At the beginning of the trial, DA Tracy Graham Lawson was able to convince the judge to let her talk about the charges he dismissed during the trial. It was called similar transactions. She was excited about this and was in the hallway bragging about it to Jeff Turner, who came and high-fived her in front of everyone like it was a "got him" moment. Turner was still looking for a way to become sheriff and was hoping this indictment would yield a conviction which would allow him to leave the chairman's seat and run.

The DA brought in witness after witness, trying to convince a jury that driving my patrol car out of town made me a RICO-organized crime lord, using the sheriff's office as a criminal enterprise. It got comical. At one point, the DA brought in an out-of-state policeman I had passed, who picked me up on his tagged reader and did not stop me; to prove I went out of town in my assigned vehicle. When Steve Frey cross-examined the officer, he asked him if he ran the plate on my police vehicle. The officer replied yes. Then Steve Frey asked him, did the car come back stolen? The whole courtroom erupted with laughter, and I turned and looked at the DA to see if she got the joke. She did not. She looked like a jackass. It was obvious that she was really expecting me to take a plea and never believed they would have to be in a trial with the nonsense they had convinced a grand jury to indict me for.

Jonathan Newton, the man employed as my public information officer who resigned after we investigated him for taking kickbacks from a printer was called to testify and that turned into a clown show as well. He testified very differently to what he said in his taped interview with investigators. Even though this interview was videotaped showing him asking for a deal after he admitted I had nothing to do with his kickback scheme, he lied on the stand and said I could not afford to pay him what he was worth, so I told him to get a kickback. I guess the deal they made for him was to lie to see if they could get me convicted. As his testimony went on, he started taking off his jacket while rolling up his shirt and drinking plenty of water as his mouth got dry from lying. Then all of a sudden, he broke down and started crying while admitting to tax evasion. It was classic.

When the jury acquitted me of all charges, the look on the DA's face was also classic. The whole crew of attorneys who had gotten elected as a slate to the offices of sheriff, the DA, and the Solicitor were mad and showed it. If they could have gotten me convicted, they were planning on getting Jeff Turner in with a special election, but that option was now gone.

After the acquittal, the DA dropped the charges on Jonathan Newton, even though he admitted to stealing money from the sheriff's office and admitted to tax evasion on the stand. This proved the case was only about me and not about justice, because they let the real criminal walk. After this "drats, foiled again" moment, all of them started looking and plotting a new way to get me out of office and would continue to do so for the next decade. As you will read, Newton and everyone that was involved in this indictment plot back in 2008 were involved in the indictment that put me here in prison from where I now write this book.

Jonathan Newton swore he would go and become an attorney so he could come back after me legally. But here is where that gets interesting. When Newton came to work at the sheriff's office, his application confirmed he had a high school education and never stepped foot on a college campus. Newton moved out of state to Maryland, where no one would question this, and a year later, was enrolled in law school saying he had a bachelor's degree from

Thomas Edison University, an online college. I got wind a news reporter interviewed Newton asking him to produce proof that he graduated from that college but he could not. He told the reporter he was worried about where this interview was going to go and that he was losing sleep. For some reason, this story never aired.

After the acquittal, I made the most powerful decision in my career that eliminated all distractions and resulted in making the sheriff's office the most effective crime-fighting agency in Georgia: the decision to ignore the media.

Chapter 8

The Press, the Prosecutors, and the Robert Ford Syndrome

J ust like a professional boxer ignores the screams of the crowd from fans and foes alike in the arena so that he can concentrate on knocking out his opponent, I choose to ignore the press while I concentrated on knocking out the crime in "my county." I have not interviewed with the media in over a decade. No interviews, no press conferences, nothing. Yet I won three elections and endorsed candidates to help them win their seats as well.

It has been said that the number one biggest fear of all time is the fear of public speaking. This is not completely accurate. The real number one fear people have is the fear of what others will say or think about them after they have given a speech. This is why the media has such a psychological hold of perceived power over so many people, especially those in appointed and elected leadership positions. The media takes advantage of this while leaders elected and appointed cower down to the media and make their decisions based on the fear of how they might be portrayed, or how truth can be spun with the intent to gain ratings. So great is this fear, I once had a local politician tell me that he tries to read tomorrow's headlines today, before he makes any decision which proved how distracted elected and appointed leaders are hoping to either please or avoid media scrutiny. I was too busy doing my job of running criminals out of "my county" to read or worry about any headlines that were not related to my mission.

Leaders also feel obligated to clear their names when the press makes false allegations against them. As a matter of fact, one of the main tactics the media uses is to run a story on someone making accusations that they already know are false, just to reel them into coming out to defend themselves. If the leader does not give an interview, the media will try to intimidate them by making it look like they are avoiding them because it must be true. They know most people fear what others hear or think about them, so this tactic is almost guaranteed to work to get their mark to agree to an interview. Those who fall for this should ask themselves, when has going to the teller of a lie ever cleared up a lie? Another tactic they use is to tell their intended target they want to do a good story on them about something unrelated so they can get them on camera to ask them about the story they are really trying to do, then, never air the story they claimed they were there for. This usually is guaranteed to work because most people who fear something bad will be said about them crave something good to be said. That is why good or bad—even if you save the world from aliens—it is best not to interview with the media.

The fear-based mentality of what others might think gives the media way too much perceived psychological power over ap-pointed and elected leaders affecting their ability to make effective decisions out of fear of media-spun controversy. As a result, most elected leaders hesitate or take no action at all, and in the world of law enforcement, wavering or doing nothing results in high crime. High crime results in officers and civilians getting injured or killed.

With the technology that exists now in the realm of social media, I am still amazed at how much control leaders in elected and appointed positions allow the media to exert over them. Everyone now has the power to get their message out without the help of the mainstream media. As a matter of fact, social media has put the power of media in everyone's hands to reach far more people than mainstream media can. In Atlanta, the local TV station with the most reach had about 180 thousand viewers at prime time. At the sheriff's office, through just the use of a text message and social media platforms, we were able to reach over 300 thousand people at the touch of a button anytime we wanted, instead of waiting and hoping the media would air the story on the six o'clock news. Also, by communicating directly to the public, we did not have to deal with the spin games the mainstream media play for ratings. The power of social media has taken away the need for mainstream media to reach your intended audience, so the need to waste time with the media is null and void. Once elected officials finally figure out they don't need the media to get or stay elected, they can begin to do their jobs without the distraction of the media, which has kept them suspended and paralyzed in fear for so long.

The truth about the media is that they are private corporations making profit from advertisements. They are not a constitutional office or law enforcement agency, nor do they have any law enforcement investigative powers such as a subpoena or search warrant. The media does have rights under the First Amendment for freedom of the press, which they believe gives them a license to lie. However, that does not negate the Fifth Amendment right all citizens have that, even when questioned by government officials, they are not required to answer any questions.

Let's think about this for a second, if a local, state, or federal law enforcement agency wants to question you, the Constitution says you have a right to remain silent. If they can't make you talk to them, why does everyone think they have to speak to the press? It is perhaps the greatest "Jedi mind trick" I've ever seen. If people would stop wasting time trying to justify themselves to the press and do a media strike, it would no doubt put them out of business.

There is a documentary on Netflix called *Trial by Media* I recommend. It documents how the media will try to move the needle on the outcome of a criminal trial or election by "creative reporting." The media creates their reports based on who they like or dislike and believe the public should take their word for it and vote for who they like. The media becomes very angry and vindictive when the voters think for themselves and vote for who they want, rather than who the media recommends or endorse.

We must always remember that the objective of media is not there to get the truth, they're there to get a "good" story. They are the epitome and the creator of the cliché, "Let's not let the facts get in the way of a good story." If the story is not good enough, they will *make* it good enough. Or if they don't make up a story, they will lie by omission as opposed to lying by commission—meaning they will leave out the important details that could clear an incident up just to keep the story going. Just like prosecutors can lie to a grand jury without consequences, the media has a license to lie to the public with impunity as well.

When leaders in law enforcement lead in fear of the media, they will always second guess every decision until they don't make any decisions at all. If you lead in fear, you will spread fear, because whatever mentality the leader has, his organization has. If your deputies become fearful, they become hesitant, which often leads them to taking no action at all. We saw this when officers and their leader did not make entry into an active shooter situation while a gunman was inside killing kids at an elementary school. They were not scared of him. They were afraid of scrutiny from the media if anything went wrong, and of the prosecutors who would try to get in on the show to indict them if they saw the media come against them. These types of prosecutors are psychologically married to the media because they both suffer from the same syndrome known as the Robert Ford Syndrome.

The Robert Ford Syndrome

What is the Robert Ford Syndrome? To understand what that syndrome is, you must know who Robert Ford is. Most people have never heard of Robert Ford, which is what makes this syndrome so dangerous—because the people who have the syndrome usually have it because no one knows or cares who they are either.

Robert Ford is the man who shot Jesse James in the back and killed him. The story is kind of sad, in a way, because Robert Ford was a fan of Jesse James prior to killing him. In fact, he wanted to *be* Jesse James. The one thing historians agree on is that Robert Ford felt that if he killed Jesse James, his name and fame would rise to the same level if not higher. This proved to be a false calculation. Jesse James received more accolades in death than Robert Ford received in life and death. Jessie James's body was taken on tour and people stood in line and paid a dime just to view his remains. This did not happen for Robert Ford, even when he was still alive. On Robert Ford's tombstone, it reads, "Here lies the man who shot and killed Jessie James." This tombstone epitomized the syndrome which gives those who suffer from it the need to say they did something to someone famous to feel they share a part of that individual's fame. The Robert Fords of the world are still alive and well today and putting them in office as prosecutors is just as dangerous as giving Robert Ford a gun when Jessie James's back was turned.

When prosecutors have the Robert Ford Syndrome, the most dangerous place for anyone is between them and a news camera. They love press conferences and will look for any reason to indict a well-known or high-profile person to bring attention to themselves. They especially love going after elected officials and cops, to the point they will ignore all the rapes, robberies, and murders in their jurisdictions and use much of the money in their budget to make up cases on high-profile individuals just so they can be a frequent guest on the six o'clock news. They also get involved in politics to control the outcomes of elections by indicting officials not in their party or not in their political clique. Even if there is no sound legal basis to indict their target, that is no problem for them because as you have read from my first case as an example, they can indict anyone for anything with no checks and balances to hold them accountable for lying to grand juries rather by omission or commission.

Prosecutors don't have to get a warrant from a judge who is trained on the elements of the law. All they must do is convince the majority of twelve untrained citizens who believe they are being given all of the facts by a prosecutor who more often than not is coercing them to vote to indict their intended target. Prosecutors can lie to a grand jury easily because a defendant nor his defense is allowed to be there. They can conveniently leave out the facts that would make a jury not consider indicting the target. That is why it is said that a DA can convict a ham sandwich, and they will indict a ham sandwich if they think they can get a press conference out of it to satisfy their much-craved fifteen seconds of fame. My high-profile career as sheriff would keep me as the apple of the eyes of reporters and DAs who are infected by the Robert Ford Syndrome.

Selective Prosecution

When I first joined the Clayton County Police, an officer on a traffic stop, while holding suspects at gunpoint waiting for backup, accidentally shot one of the suspects. He was not criminally charged. Why? Because it was an accident and there was no criminal intent. The first deputy ever killed in the line of duty at the Clayton County sheriff's office was killed in an accidental shooting during SWAT training by another deputy. The deputy who shot and killed him was never criminally charged. Why? Because it was an accident and there was no criminal intent.

In 2015, while going through a training scenario with a friend, I too had an accidental shooting which did not result in death. A warrant was taken out on me for reckless conduct, and I was brought before a grand jury by prosecutors to see if they could get the charges upgraded to aggravated assault. Ironically, while all of this was going on, a man who was looking at a gun at a pawn shop in Clayton County accidentally shot his girlfriend. This incident garnered no charges and no media. Why? Because it was an accident with no criminal intent, and he was not a public figure.

The reason I'm bringing up these accidental shootings that are like mine is not because I believe the individuals who committed the accidents should be charged. I am not saying I should not have been charged. I am bringing it up because I believe if you are going to charge people for accidental shootings, charge everyone. And if you are not going to charge everyone involved in an accidental shooting, then don't charge anyone at all. To only charge the people you think can get you on TV is selective prosecution spurred by the Robert Ford Syndrome.

During my incident, my attorney told me that the DA had to indict me so he could save face in the media to show I was being held to "a higher standard." What is "a higher standard"? The truth of the matter is the "higher standard" media and prosecutors try to hold a select few too is the malarkey they use to justify selective prosecution. They also use it to have something they perceive as memorable to say at their press conferences. Prosecutors love press conferences because they hope it will make them famous and revered and, of course, get them reelected. There, they can rant and rave about how no man is above the law and how they're going to hold everyone with a name or title to "a higher standard" instead of holding them to the same standard they hold others who can't garner them a press conference. I don't believe there is any man above the law—including me—but I also don't believe it is fair to hold any man below the law as well. I don't believe that anyone should be held to a higher or lower standard. I believe everyone should be held to the same standard. To say people can have an accidental shooting and not be charged because they don't hold a title or have a name is hypocritical.

Selective prosecution is one of the main things that's wrong with how prosecutors are allowed to operate with impunity. A DA can decide who to prosecute and who not to prosecute and this discretion is often abused to let who they want get away with crimes while they enforce the same crimes only on who they select. Under this system of prosecution, a person can be prosecuted for a crime while another person can do the exact same crime or something more egregious and a prosecutor can simply decide not to prosecute simply because of relationships, friendships, or political favors. Prosecutors, just like judges, who write opinions contrary to their prior rulings if they want to rule against a particular individual, can simply make up a reason why they should not prosecute someone who has committed the same crime if not worse. Until this glitch in the system is fixed, there will never be consistency and fairness in our criminal justice system.

Perhaps one day, prosecutors with the Robert Ford Syndrome will hold themselves to "a higher standard."

The True Cause of Rising Crime

Do social and economic challenges affect crime? Of course. Did Covid-19 contribute to the crime epidemic our nation now faces? Perhaps indirectly due to the fear of leaders to act out of fear of media scrutiny. Just like a good doctor looks for the root cause of disease, so must we identify the root cause of the crime epidemic, and that certainly is not Covid-19. The root cause of our crime epidemic that most leaders in law enforcement fear to admit is that law enforcement is now terrified to do their jobs due to the fear of the press and prosecutors. Can you blame them for fearing that if the political wind blows against them, they can end up where I now sit? The politics of the media and prosecutors have not only caused early retirements and low recruitment, but the officers who remain now often hesitate to do their jobs or refrain as much as possible from doing anything, which gives criminals free reign. Law enforcement is fearful to do what it takes to protect themselves or the public knowing they will be second-guessed by the press who will report in a way that incites riots, regardless of if the use of force is justified or not and prosecutors will be standing by to indict them to get their claim to fame from it. This crazy culture created by the press and prosecutors with the Robert Ford Syndrome has caused law enforcement who are good at doing their jobs to start retiring early, looking for other professions, and has made it difficult to recruit new officers, not willing to risk becoming a sacrificial lamb for these two entities. After my indictment and suspension from office, not only were four inmates murdered in the jail, but the murder rate in Clayton County rose to an all-time high. Because prosecutors took the position of defending and coming to rescue criminals from me, the criminals took my prosecution as a win for them, and took advantage of it at the cost of lives on the streets and the jail.

This case, among others, is why many cops are afraid to do their jobs and a lot of them silently protest by simply not doing their jobs. This is a major problem and is the reason why law enforcement is not able to be as effective as they could be in reducing, preventing, and controlling crime. What is the solution?

The solution is simple but far from easy. First, law enforcement leaders must become strong enough to ignore the media and create their own media outlets to keep the public informed that is transparently free of the mainstream media spin. Next, law enforcement leaders will have to lobby for laws to create checks and balances to regulate prosecutors from abusing their power to indict and selectively prosecute for political reasons.

Our elected and appointed leaders in law enforcement must thicken their skins and begin to develop a lion's mentality if they are ever going to be able to control the lion's den of emboldened criminals the press and prosecutors have created. A lion's mentality that does not fear opinions of media spun stories to prevent them from taking action to protect the lives of the public. What is a lion's mentality? To understand the lion's mentality, you have to understand why the lion is the king of the jungle. It's not because he's the biggest—that's the elephant. It can't be because he's the fastest—that's the cheetah. It certainly isn't because he is the tallest. The giraffe is the tallest. Even the tallest giraffe thinks to run when he sees a lion, but when the lion sees the giraffe, he thinks of lunch. The lion is king because of his mentality, and that is why lions don't lose sleep over the opinions of giraffes.

Chapter 9

War on Crime

J ust like a good chess player moves his front pieces strategically forward to keep pressure on his opponent, so does a crime-fighting strategist keep pressure on the criminal element to force them into defense. If a chess player stays on the defense and only responds when his opponent makes aggressive moves, he will get locked in, overcome, and will soon lose the game. However, if a chess player makes his defense a good offense, the opponent will never have time to attack his king and will stay on defense. So it is with the strategy of fighting crime.

But there is another game that would influence and teach me how to effectively prevent, control, and reduce crime on another level, the ancient Chinese game called "Go." Sun Tzu and Chairman Mao of China were avid players of Go and it was with its precepts and strategies that Mao conquered China and Sun Tzu became a sought-after General for his ability to win wars. There were shoguns in Japan who would not accept a samurai unless the warrior played and understood the precepts of Go.

Legend has it, after studying wars over the history of mankind going as far back as the Napoleonic-era that no general employing a chess strategy has ever won against a general employing a Go strategy, citing Vietnam as an example. Some argue that Go is superior to chess, but I see it differently as I am an avid lover and student of both games for several reasons. To me, chess and Go are the perfect yin and yang balance, giving me multiple options in my strategic arsenal. Chess is linear while Go is circular. In chess, the game takes form with two opposing armies facing each other. Go is formless, starting with an empty board. Chess simulates conventional warfare while Go simulates unconventional warfare. In chess, you capture one piece at a time with the goal of capturing the king. In Go, you can capture multiple pieces at a time, but the true masters capture none and still win by simply controlling the territory on the board. Both games gave me effective strategies to fight crime. From the game of chess, I would checkmate key figures of crime in "my county." From the game of Go, I would fight crime effectively by simply taking control of territories whether it was a high crime area or the jail.

I mainly applied this concept of controlling a territory when it came to the war on drugs in "my county." The majority of law enforcement fight the war on drugs only using a chess strategy of capturing one king (pin) at a time and locking them up for a ridiculous amount of time, only to have someone else take their "crown" and continue to sell drugs. Let's face it, if using this strategy alone worked, we would no longer have a drug problem. But by also applying the main precept of Go, of *controlling* the territory in addition, as opposed to just capturing the king (pins), we eliminated all open-air drug dealing and were able to control drug trafficking significantly more than anyone in the history of Clayton County. Capturing king (pins) is a long, arduous process requiring search warrants, surveillance, and a lot of other complicated stuff that can take up to a year or more. Meanwhile, people are getting killed and suffering from the lack of quality of life that having a drug house in their neighborhood brings. We simply started closing drug houses down by controlling the territory. Here's how.

I've always asked, if everyone in the neighborhood knows where the drug houses are and the police know where the drug houses are, why are there still drug houses? I knew of drug houses in Clayton County before I became sheriff that stayed operational for years, even though it was common knowledge they sold drugs. Every now and then the narcotics division would get a search warrant and hit the house and take someone into custody but usually the house would be back up and running the same week—if not the same day. It made no sense whatsoever.

My philosophy is if everyone knows where people are selling drugs, including law enforcement, the drugs at that location should no longer be served. If I got wind that there was a drug house, I made sure there would no longer be a drug house. As wild and simple as it may sound, most of the drug houses we closed were not done with drug investigation search warrants. I just used a simple, common sense, Old Western sheriff strategy that worked back then and continues to work now. I call it my "get out of town by sundown" strategy and in the law enforcement world, it is called a "knock and talk." When I retook the sheriff's office back in 2013, Southern Springs apartments off of Mt. Zion Road with a one-way entrance behind QuikTrip was a half-abandoned complex that had been seized by drug dealers of which you could see a mob of them standing outside. Before I took office at midnight on New Year's Eve, I road back there and told them to be gone before I became sheriff again. They did and the complex was later shut down and condemned. When I would learn of or observe a house with suspected drug activity, I simply went and knocked on the door, spoke with them, and told them I needed them to leave Clayton County and find somewhere else to sell drugs. And that is exactly what most of them did. For the ones that didn't, I simply put a marked patrol car strategically where anyone coming to buy drugs from them could see the car. By this simple technique, we were essentially putting the drug houses "in check" — using chess terminology — and staying in front of houses 24/7 until we achieved checkmate when they moved out.

If the terrain was not suitable for the chess checkmate strategy, we would simply seize the outer perimeter by controlling the territory with safety road checks and tag readers both stationary and on patrol vehicles. For some reason, wherever there is drug trafficking, there are usually a lot of traffic infractions which are dangerous for all in the area, especially children. When situations like that occur, it allows us to do safety road checks. People who like to buy drugs do not like going through road checks. This is because they may be wanted or in possession of illegal contraband, not to mention their tag might be expired or they might have no insurance on the car. If the area they're going into to buy drugs has a lot of safety road checks, they cease doing business there. As a result, the drug dealer's business dries up and he has to pack up and move elsewhere. Problem solved!

Control the territory and you control the crime. It is not hard, and it works anywhere, anytime, every time. No one had to go and serve a long prison term, the drug operation was shut down, and the little old ladies were able to enjoy the homes they purchased, to live in peace as they were supposed to.

Another method used to control the territory in "my county" was to mark our territory. Gangs mark their territory by placing graffiti in different locations. As long as their graffiti is allowed to stay up, it shows their dominance and the apathy and lack of control by leadership where this is allowed. A ride through downtown Atlanta, which sits right next to "my county" in some areas, is like a ride through graffiti land. Once, when I went downtown for lunch, I saw several individuals putting graffiti up in broad daylight in a highly trafficked area with no apparent fear of law enforcement. Not in "my county." I had my S.K.I.P. team (Sheriff's Kleen Initiative Program) go on a graffiti-patrol every day and remove any graffiti found until we had zero graffiti in Clayton County. While not allowing gangs to mark any territory in "my county," we instead marked the territory ourselves! At every entrance into the county, we had signs with the sheriff's emblem on it that said, "Welcome to Clayton County where criminals enter at their own risk" as a deterrent and warning to thugs to either act right in our jurisdiction, or turn around and go elsewhere. At the main entrance of the county, we had a huge sheriff's office flag as another warning that they were entering territory controlled by us and not by gangs. It worked!

The Go concept of controlling the territory is also how I was able to gain control over the jail in such a short period of time. By simply cutting off all entries and exits for employees to one entrance and searching everyone regardless of status every time they enter the jail while having it video recorded, we were able to eliminate any contraband from entering the jail. We also kept the jail free from graffiti inside and out, marking our territory there as well. At the entrance to the jail were signs that said, "Welcome to Georgia's toughest para-military jail, better known as 'the Hill-ton.'" This set the tone upon entry that the jail was a place of order and discipline. Control the territory and you control the crime—regardless of where the territory is. Controlling the territory is the overall macro strategy to effectively prevent and reduce crime, but there are intricate strategies that work for crime prevention and reduction as well.

How to Reduce Violent Crime

Just like there are different strategies on the chess and Go boards, there are various sub-strategies when it comes to preventing and controlling violent crime. Again, the underlying strategy is always to control the territory, but knowing exactly what to control that criminals need to operate is very important.

There are two things' criminals need to commit crimes, trans-portation and guns. A criminal must have transportation to get to the crime scene and escape from the crime scene. Public transpor-tation simply won't work to escape from the scene after they burglarize someone's home or business or commit some form of a robbery. Criminals know they can't drive their mother's or girl-friend's car to commit crimes because law enforcement will run the tag and ask the owner who was in possession of the car, leading back to them. So, criminals have no option but to steal cars to commit crimes. If they don't, they can't get to the crime scene and, most importantly, can't escape the crime scene. Wherever cars are being stolen, all types of crimes—up to and including murder—are going to occur. If you target where the most cars are being stolen and effectively stop it, you will make the criminals in your jurisdiction stranded, and a stranded criminal is an ineffective criminal because he does not have the transportation needed for him to go to work.

But law enforcement must be able to pursue the individuals in the stolen cars to stop them from preventing further crimes to truly be effective. Unfortunately, this is where the politics of the media and prosecutors hamper law enforcement as well.

Virtually all law enforcement has adopted a no-chase policy due to the fear of the media and Robert Ford Syndrome prosecutors. Law enforcement is rightfully terrified because if that chase ends in a wreck and someone is injured or dies, the media and the prosecutors are not interested in the fact that it is the criminals who caused this by risking the public's life so they could escape. Instead, they target law enforcement, blaming them for the accidents when it was just their intent to do their jobs to apprehend criminals. If a study is done of how many people are robbed or killed by suspects in stolen cars, someone will see the light on why they need to be pursued. Pursued within reason of course. Suspects should not be pursued through a school zone during school hours or in areas where there is heavy pedestrian traffic if possible. The latest technology and tactics to end the chase as soon as possible should always be deployed to minimize risk. Unfortunately, risk can only be minimized but never eliminated. But to simply act as a deer in headlights, doing nothing and letting criminals escape capture out of fear, is the number one reason jurisdictions are unable to get control of their crime and often those who are allowed to escape capture in the name of saving lives end up taking lives in the crimes they are allowed to commit because they don't have to worry about being pursued. Instead of blaming cops for pursuing criminals as they are trained to do, politicians, prosecutors, and media could better spend their time supporting the creation of legislation to crack down on criminals who endanger the public by putting their lives at risk so they can escape capture after victimizing innocent citizens. Instead, the media tries these officers in the court of public opinion and prosecutors, looking to make a name for themselves, focus more on prosecuting the cops rather than the criminals they were pursuing. The media and Robert Ford prosecutors have made it easier for criminals to commit their crimes and made it hard for cops to do their jobs.

The other thing you have to stop from getting into criminals' hands is guns. How do most criminals get guns? From breaking into houses and cars where people leave guns unsecured. Car break-ins and burglaries are predicated crimes that breed violent crimes, much like a pond of water in the grass can breed mosquitoes.

Take away criminals abilities to steal guns and cars and you leave them stranded and unarmed. You can usually tell where the robbing and killing will take place just by looking at where the increase is in car break-ins and burglaries. Wherever I see a rash of these crimes, I ascertain how many firearms were taken during these crimes. If it is a significant amount, I saturate that area with targeted patrols to take back those guns from the criminals carry-ing them. How do you stop car break-ins, burglaries, and auto theft? You control the territory. How do you control the territory? You place marked and unmarked patrol cars, flock cameras, and road checks strategically where they need to be, making it hard not only to commit these crimes but also hard not to get caught. Control the territory and you control the crime.

How to Reduce Domestic Violence

A lot of law enforcement leaders are quick to use the excuse that domestic violence murders and assaults are something no one can control. They especially use this excuse if they have a rise in murder rate and many are domestic related. The same strategy of controlling a territory when dealing with drug dealers, burglars, and car thieves applies to domestic violence as well. To deal with this, we created a stalking unit whose motto was to "stalk the stalkers," employing a Go and chess strategy to put stalkers on the defense.

If a woman gets a temporary restraining order because someone is constantly stalking her, that piece of paper alone, signed by a judge, does not stop the problem. But if we put surveillance by her house and wait for her stalker to drive by or put the stalker under surveillance so we can catch him in the act, we control the territory.

Our unit received various awards over the years from different domestic violence advocate groups. We simply took the fight to the criminals instead of waiting for the criminals to take the first shot of injuring or killing their intended victims. No rocket science needed, just common sense and strategy of war by controlling the territory.

In addition to the strategies surrounding controlling the territory, there are other common sense things leaders need to do with the law enforcement team to make sure they are effective in reducing crime. Number one, you must have deputies physically capable of protecting themselves before they can protect others. They have to actually be able to physically engage with suspects who run and resist arrest for them to be the protectors and not the victims. You must make sure your deputies are well-trained and well-armed. You don't want someone coming to your county with a rifle and owning a situation taking the lives of defenseless people until the SWAT team can arrive. Every last one of my deputies was armed and trained with rifles so that if a situation like that ever occurred, we had more than enough firepower to deal with that person to stop him from killing innocent people. Also, you've got to make your officers work when criminals work. Crime fighting is not a nine-to-five job with weekends and holidays off. You've got to have people out on the streets on nights, weekends, and holidays. If not, the criminals will rule the street during the non-banking hours while you and all your deputies are home relaxing with families and friends. Control the territory and you control the crime.

The Truth about Community Policing

To really understand what actually works to control crime, we also have to clearly define what does not work and why.

I regret to be the bearer of bad news, but there comes a time when you have to tell your nieces and nephews that there is no tooth fairy and that they are going to have to floss, brush, and get a job if they still want spending money. Community policing does not reduce crime. Community policing has value, but not in controlling and reducing crime. Its value is mostly in gaining and maintaining a rapport so that some members in the community will perhaps feel comfortable giving you information. All the effective cops did this long before the community policing term was ever coined. There is no statistical data that shows that when the police record themselves doing dancing videos, shaving homeless people, breastfeeding babies, playing with Barbie dolls with little girls, and crying at press conferences, to "show we are human too," has any effect on reducing crime. However, because of the fear of the media and prosecutors with the Robert Ford effect, most law enforcement leaders hide behind and relish in community policing, doing very little else.

During my first term as sheriff, I attended a symposium in which a beloved Atlanta rapper Killer Mike was in attendance. There were a lot of law enforcement officials there, including Jeff Turner who was the police chief at that time. When Turner spoke about his community policing plans for Clayton County, Killer Mike said something I'll never forget: "You know we all laugh at "Officer Friendly" on the streets, right?" The room got silent. Turner had no response. It went over his head as big as it was.

Killer Mike was right.

Hardened thugs do not stop raping, robbing, and murdering because they see the police making a concerted effort to stage being "nice guys" by playing with baby dolls and crying on TV at press conferences. It is a green light for them to act like a fool. If community policing actually reduced crime, then all of the violent cities that focus on hug-a-thug feel-good programs should have the lowest crime rate.

Let me be clear, Clayton County is not Mayberry. Andy Griffith and Barney Fife would never be able to deal with the type of thugs we have in Clayton County. We don't have offenders like Otis who turns himself in and locks himself up every time he gets drunk. But we did have robbers and murderers who turned themselves in because they feared my specialized squads created to sweep the streets free of their kind.

I used to frequently have very harsh conversations with known violent criminals who were acting out. If I quoted the lyrics from the *Barney* song to them, they would not have stopped assaulting old ladies in groceries stores, vandalizing their mother's homes, and running women off of the road. I reserved the Barney talk for their victims and the church mothers who baked me sweet potato pies.

Just like a drill instructor has tough conversations with recruits out of line, so have I with criminals. I cannot remember a week that went by when I did not tell one of them that if they did not cease acting out in a violent way that endangered the public, I wanted them gone from "my county." It worked and I don't apologize for not being nicer to violent criminals. Nowhere in the constitution does it say that talking tough to criminals is a violation of their constitutional rights. Nowhere has any statistical data shown that talking nicer to criminals helps lower crime. Did it scare criminals to hear directly from me that their conduct was unacceptable and would not be tolerated? I certainly hope so. One thing we know, it worked, and it worked well. If criminals are not afraid of the sheriff in your county, you don't have a sheriff, you have elected a community policing politician. Sheriffs are supposed to make their counties undesirable for criminals to want to play around in.

Did I give to the poor, feed the hungry, and clothe the naked? I certainly did, but it had nothing to do with a community policing program to try to prove to the media or anyone else I'm a nice guy. The focus of my job as sheriff and the focus of law enforcement should never be feel-good programs. The focus is to protect the good people from the bad guys by taking the fight to them before they can take their crimes to their victims. Law enforcement must refocus on this priority if we are going to control crime once and for all. I am not going to judge or criticize the officers who are deep into the officer-friendly community policing trend. But let me be clear, when it came down to doing my job of cleaning up the streets in "my county," I did not have time to play with dolls.

Chapter 10

The Atlanta Riots

T he Atlanta Riots were the epitome of all I have written about thus far regarding the dangers of the media, Robert Ford prosecutors, and the unrealistic officer-friendly community policing philosophy. The media tries to incite riots in all police use of force cases, whether the use of force is justified or not. At the end of the day, even in situations where everyone is 100 percent in agreement the use of force is excessive and the leadership takes every action they can to correct the problem, the media is still going to try to instigate a riot so they can have a story to cover. The media is the true catalyst of riots. If they were truly concerned with public safety, they would not put out unconfirmed and partial information just to flare up emotional confusion.

Just like prosecutors selectively prosecute, so does the media engage in selective reporting. Out of the four unarmed suspects my deputies shot during my tenure as sheriff, three of them were white. Not once did the media do a report on the three unarmed white suspects that were shot. Did they not care about them because they are white or did not report it because they didn't think they could incite a riot reporting white; unarmed suspects were getting shot by my deputies? They did report on the unarmed black suspect who was shot, and of course, our Robert Ford Syndrome DA indicted the deputy who just happened to be black as well. They later had to drop the charges, because it was determined his use of force was justified.

Protesters and Rioters

There are two different sets of individuals who show up at a demonstration: protesters and rioters. Protesters are those who want to express themselves and articulate their voices to right a wrong they want to see fixed. Rioters are just the thugs who want to see the city burn. Rioters really don't care about the issues the peaceful protesters are trying to articulate. They are just looking for an excuse to steal and act out. Rioters' destructive behavior should not be entertained, not even for a second. Assaulting officers in other jurisdictions who have nothing to do with what a different officer did wrong in another state is *not* going to address what that officer did. It is just an excuse to assault officers and act out. Burning a business down of an entrepreneur who is not even involved in law enforcement does not address the issue either. Rioters just use the situation as an excuse to be destructive. Proof of this is that the same rioters will show up after a natural disaster and start looting too. The minute they rear their heads, they need to be stopped. But thanks to the media and prosecutors, law enforcement is terrified to do what they need to do to stop the rioters who show up at these protests because they know the media will make it look as if they are persecuting the legitimate protesters. They also fear that the prosecutors who want to look good to the media will follow up with indictments just to get on TV. As a result, riots that could have been stopped or prevented the minute any pre-attack indicator was shown are allowed to get dangerously out of control, resulting in death and destruction. So it was with the Atlanta riots.

How the Riot Started

The day the Atlanta riots started was one of the rare days I was watching TV. The riots had not yet occurred at that point when I started watching the protest. What I saw initially gave me a funny feeling something bad was about to happen. I noticed none of the Atlanta officers had any riot gear or looked prepared for a riot. No doubt this was because they were instructed to take the hug a thug officer-friendly community policing approach to the demonstration, not considering the rioters who were sure to show up to mingle in with the legitimate protesters.

Later, I saw the Atlanta police chief walking through the crowd doing the officer-friendly community policing thing, talking to people in the demonstration thinking she could maintain the peace by being friendly and pleasant. She had already filmed a video and put it out to the public, telling everyone she understood why everyone was angry about George Floyd and that everyone had a right to be angry. I knew her heart was in the right place, but in situations like that, there's nothing anyone can say that's going to quell those who choose to be violent because of it. I knew it was a waste of time negotiating with rioters and it was not going to work. Officer-friendly strategies do not make violent people stand down, they encourage them to stand up. The only thing violent and destructive rioters understand is a show of force.

As the police chief walked through the crowd, one of the rioters threw a water bottle at her. I knew right then, in that instant, how this situation was handled from that moment would determine whether the city would spiral out of control. Throwing a water bottle at a police chief is a pre-attack indicator of what is to come. If they're bold enough that they would throw something at the highest-ranking official, they'll be bold enough to do anything. If they are not stopped right then and there to establish control, you have given them the greenlight that they can get away with anything.

The chief did nothing, and her officers stood down.

The whole demonstration should have been shut down at that moment for the safety of the entire city as well as the peaceful pro-testors, but no one had the heart to make that kind of call and follow through at the risk of the media spin. Would shutting everything down at that moment have made everyone happy? Of course not, and the media would have spun it negatively, but it would have prevented the death and destruction that occurred. There is no way to make everyone happy, but you can always keep everyone safe if you take preemptive action and take it with expediency.

Right after that bottle was thrown and nothing was done to ad-dress it, that was the catalyst of everything. Within minutes, glasses started being broken and a man appeared on top of a patrol car with a shield from inside of the car, showing that he was bold enough to break inside the police car with cops standing there. The man then began to set something on fire in his hands while the media filmed, and the cops stood by and did nothing. Then the patrol car went up in flames.

After that patrol car was burned, more police cars were set on fire and the city began spiraling more and more out of control. APD was way over their head, not because they could not handle it, but because they were not *allowed* to handle it the way it should have been done from the beginning due to fear of the politics, press, and prosecutors. The mayor did a press conference and made a passionate mother-like speech for everyone to go home. I'm sure she meant well, but that wasn't going to work either. I've spent thirty years of my life dealing with violent people and I can tell you, if a magic tongue could talk every violent individual down, we could just take all the weapons from police officers, and they should just be able to go and talk through every violent situation. As a hostage negotiator, I was trained to talk individuals down, but I was also trained to recognize when talking was not going to work and to advise SWAT to go in to stop further violence. There comes a time when law enforcement must use force and not doing so actually endangers more lives than saves them. But when you make law enforcement afraid to use force when needed, you place everyone's lives in danger. There was only one way to stop this situation and the chief of police knew it, so she finally made the call.

A couple of hours after the press conference, my phone rang, and it was the Atlanta police chief. She said they needed help and fast. I told her help was on the way if she understood we were coming to handle business and she said she understood. I put all my special force units together and clearly gave them the orders to go do what needed to be done. That is exactly what they did, and the riot was stopped.

The next day, the assistant chief called me and asked if I could send my deputies back again the next night as a follow-up and if I would attend a meeting with the police chief, mayor, and other law enforcement heads. I agreed. It turned out that other agencies who'd come to assist had also gotten their cars torched with flames. I recall the police chief asking each head of every agency how many cars they lost in the riot and the agencies would give whatever the number was. When she turned and asked me how many cars my agency lost, everyone in the room was stunned when I replied none. I did not say it in the meeting, but my commanders informed me that a lot of the rioters dispersed the moment they saw Clayton County Sheriff on the cars, essentially commenting that we were not to be played with in so many words. The rioters were not a problem for us because the job my administration had done in Clayton County set a tone that we were a no-nonsense law enforcement agency. No one thought to approach our cars and set them on fire. After the conclusion of the meeting, we agreed on what would be the plan to keep the city safe that night, and I gave the orders to my team to return and to continue to assist APD. But something would happen that night that would cause me to call my team back and tell them not to return the following morning.

Even though the second night, for the most part, was a success, another incident occurred that would be blown out of proportion by the media, politicians, and Robert Ford Syndrome prosecutors.

A group of young people in a car decided not to stop for the police when they were ordered to. Instead, they took off. The traffic in front of them stopped them from being able to escape, so officers were able to run up on foot and catch up to them. When the suspects refused to open the doors, the officers had to break the car windows to get them out of the car to arrest them and used Tasers to get them under control. Because tensions were high and politics were involved, the Mayor of Atlanta called for the immediate termination of those officers and asked for them to be criminally prosecuted. When I was made aware of this, I immediately told my deputies to return to Clayton County. The riot situation was dangerous enough and if they were going to be critiqued on their every move, fired, and prosecuted to please the media, even when they were acting within the scope of their training and the law, I did not want my deputies involved. But the problem got even deeper.

After they returned on my orders, one of my deputies was concerned he was going to be criminally prosecuted because of this incident. It turned out, my deputies were in the area when the APD officer approached the car and pulled the disorderly suspects from the car. In order to stop the suspects from driving off, and possibly injuring the public or officers, he disabled the vehicle by stabbing the tires with a pocketknife. On the news, you could see him deflating the tires and, of course, the media spin was to show it as a part of the police brutality sensation they were trying to push to keep the riots going. After watching the APD officers get fired and prosecuted for doing their jobs, he understandably figured the press and prosecutors would come looking for his head too. I assured him that if that happened, I would stand with him, and help with his criminal defense.

I was the one who instructed my deputies to use this safety tactic anyway. Approximately a month before this riot occurred, I held a meeting with my field division and explained to them I wanted to use strategies that could prevent problems before they occur. We were one of the few agencies left that still pursued vehicles when criminals tried to get away. As I have explained, to reduce crime, vehicle pursuits are a very necessary evil. In this meeting, I was trying to impart my philosophy of preventing and controlling situations upon my deputies, so they don't even occur. I explained to them I would rather see a high-speed chase not happen if possible and gave them strategies to prevent them from happening at all.

One method I taught my deputies in that meeting was that if they were looking for a suspect and located his car, and knew he had the potential to flee, I would rather see them flatten the tire and prevent him from fleeing in the vehicle, while placing the lives of the public at risk as well as theirs. I told them that the worst-case scenario in this tactic is us paying to replace a tire instead of something we can't replace—a life. Although I do not believe law enforcement should stop pursuing vehicles, when necessary, I also believe we should do everything in our power to prevent vehicle pursuits while still achieving the objective of apprehension. But in the political climate with law enforcement, the ounce of prevention worth a pound of cure is now ridiculed in the media and prosecuted by political prosecutors.

The intent of my deputy stabbing the tire of the vehicle was to stop them from fleeing to prevent anyone from getting hurt. But that's not the way it was portrayed in the media and if they had identified my deputy, there is no doubt he would have been criminally charged just as they wrongfully charged those Atlanta police officers who were simply doing their jobs. Eventually, those officers got their jobs back and they were cleared of the criminal prosecution because their use of force was justified. But at what cost to the officers and their families just to satisfy the media for a political show. The use of force, even when justified, is not pretty, but just because it is not pretty does not mean it is unjustified. The Eleventh Circuit Court articulated this when they said, "Everything that stinks does not violate the constitution." Nothing these officers did was outside the scope of their training, policy, or law, just as nothing I did was either. But if it is prosecutable in the media's court of public opinion, that is all prosecutors need. These types of prosecutors who prosecute just to satisfy the media in exchange for fifteen seconds of fame at a press conference are truly the root cause of our crime epidemic. That was exactly what happened in this case, and the fiasco would not end there.

Police Shooting at Wendy's

On June 12, 2020, two Atlanta Police Officers were involved in the shooting that led to the death of Rayshard Brooks. These officers were called to the parking lot of a Wendy's fast-food restaurant in reference to a man who had fallen asleep in a car. They got him out of the car to check if he was DUI. Please note, he was compliant the whole time, up to the point they told him he was under arrest and were about to place handcuffs on him. He even moved in such a way as if he was going to comply with the arrest. But before they could put the cuffs on, Brooks began fighting them and was able to get the best of them both. He disarmed and took one of the officer's Taser.

As he ran off, Brooks turned around and pointed the Taser at the officer as if it were a firearm. The officer drew his weapon and fired, shooting and killing Brooks. The media played the video of the shooting in their usual fashion, adding fuel to a city still on fire from the Geoge Floyd riot, and started the Monday morning quarterback fiasco they do for ratings. Everybody had an opinion of whether it was right or wrong at the expense of the officers and their families. The officers acted within the scope of law and policy. Many did not like what they saw and thought things could have been done differently, but that still doesn't make what the officers did illegal. The media did their best by adding fuel to the fire, hyping it up, to the point where the mayor jumped in on the bandwagon and demanded the two officers be fired and prosecuted for murder.

There should be no wonder why officers remain fearful and hesitant to do their jobs resulting in the domino effect of a crime wave.

Roadblock Conducted by Thugs

Due to the deadly domino effect of the media, Robert Ford prosecutors and the pressure on law enforcement to be officer-friendly community police, the out-of-control spiral continued. After the demonstrations had quieted down, I received a very interesting phone call from a friend of mine who lives in the city of Atlanta. He asked me if I knew that there was a roadblock at the Wendy's where the shooting occurred. I told him I did not, but that it was a good thing the Atlanta police were doing that. That's when he told me, it was not the police conducting the road check, it was some thugs with rifles conducting the road check.

"Are you sure about this?" I asked. "Did you just hear about this or did you actually see it with your own eyes?" I continued.

"I'm here, watching it right now," he replied, and then sent me a picture of the roadblock conducted by thugs.

I immediately asked him if he knew if anyone had called the police yet. He was not sure but had concluded that if they had, the police would have done nothing about it. So, I told him I would call the Atlanta police chief and forward the picture to him. At this time, Chief Shields had stepped down as police chief and Rodney Bryant was the new chief. As I dialed his number, I remember thinking just how out of control the city of Atlanta had gotten.

I asked Chief Bryant if he knew there were armed guys at the Wendy's holding an armed roadblock, and to check his phone for the picture I just sent him. I told the chief I did not know what his relationship was with city hall, but if they were not going to allow him to do his job and take control of the streets instead of allowing the thugs to control the streets the position was not worth it. There was no debate. He agreed and said he was going to handle it. To his credit, he did jump on top of it. I know this because a friend of mine on the SWAT team for that jurisdiction said they had been activated to shut the situation down.

The next day, I waited to hear some news about what had happened but heard absolutely nothing. I called my friend on the SWAT team to ask how it went. He told me they were told to stand down.

"Stand down?" I asked, "Why?"

My friend told me city hall had told the chief to stand down from taking any actions against the armed thugs doing the road check in case it turned into a confrontation and was hopeful that someone could go talk them down. "Okay, we'll see how this turns out," I said, knowing in my gut that this would not end well. It was not even three weeks later that one of the armed men holding that roadblock began shooting and accidentally killed an eight-year-old child in a vehicle. Had this road check been stopped when I called the chief and advised him, that eight-year-old child would be alive today. All of this is because of the political climate created by the media and Robert Ford prosecutors that have produced the officer-friendly community policing posture that allows violent criminals free reign to assault and murder.

The Irony

When George Floyd was killed by a policeman who literally refused to take his knee off Floyd's neck after he was restrained, it shocked the world. I don't know anyone in law enforcement who agreed with Chavin's use of force in this incident. This was a no-brainer. Once the restraints are placed on a suspect, anything more is excessive force. There's nothing further that can or should be done. To place a knee on the suspect, after he was restrained, and restrict his breathing, without a doubt, is excessive force. Any one of my deputies that struck, kicked, or—in one instance—pulled a gun on a suspect after they were restrained, were fired.

Ironically, I am charged with the exact federal charge Derek Chavin is charged with, on six counts, as I write this book from my prison cell. None of my alleged victims died, and none of them were injured. As a matter of fact, they were checked before and after they were restrained by nurses and checked every fifteen minutes by officers.

The Rayshard Brooks case also deals with the question of the use of restraints in the effect that the use of them preemptively could have possibly prevented the incident. Back when I was a rookie, I found myself on a call almost identical to one like Rayshard Brooks. As soon as he stepped out of the vehicle, I placed him in restraints, telling him it was for his safety and mine until I could figure out what was going on. After I located narcotics in his vehicle and told him he was under arrest, he too became combative, but it was too late because the cuffs were already on. That situation could have turned out like Rayshard Brooks had I not used the restraints preemptively.

All the major three incidents that occurred in this chapter could have been stopped, including the loss of an innocent eight-year-old child with preemptive preventative action. All of the pre-attack indicators law enforcement are trained to spot were there. If preemptive action were taken, these situations would not have gotten out of hand or may not have occurred at all. Georgia Peace Officers are still trained every year in the use of preventative restraints and the preemptive use of force but are afraid to do so because of the media and prosecutors who can indict any officer regardless of law and training if they so desire. Ask me how I know.

Chapter 11

Call in the Feds

I n the first episode of the highly acclaimed, long-running NBC series, *The Blacklist*—which aired ten seasons with 218 episodes—the villain Raymond Reddington turned himself in at the FBI headquarters. He did this of his own free will and was completely compliant. As a precaution, the FBI places him in a safety restraint chair due to their "prior knowledge" of his propensity for violence. As a matter of fact, he spends a significant amount of time in the safety restraint chair because after he gives them information, they leave the office and get into a full-fledged shootout and car crash. When they return, Raymond is still in the safety restraint chair. It is only after they feel he is not a threat that he is released from the safety restraint chair.

I bring this up because not only is this a scenario identical to the main case federal prosecutors brought against me, but it makes it obvious that no one in Hollywood or the public knew or thought the safety restraint used in this manner was a criminal act to include the FBI. This is how the public, Hollywood, and everyone else thought the safety restraint chairs were supposed to be used. And they were right because this is the manner it has been used in for as long as I can remember—which is supported by state training and the sheriff's office policy. It was only when my political enemies in two prosecutorial offices, both local and federal, were looking for anything to charge me with did the use of the safety restraint chair in this manner suddenly became illegal and a violation of civil rights. But this would become the crux of what the government would base their case on, saying the suspects I authorized to be restrained for safety were compliant instead of uncontrollably violent when they were placed in the safety restraint chair arguing that they could only be placed in the chair if they were uncontrollably violent at the time they were placed there.

If you watch the news about my restraint chair case, it will appear that seven inmates went to the FBI to complain they were being brutalized in the restraint chair and the FBI rode in on a white horse to save them from the big bad sheriff in Clayton County. After all, no man is above the law, and violent criminals need their rights protected too. And because the FBI are the brave ones who care about violent criminals just as much as they care about their victims, they had to act before more violent criminals got restrained for safety while being checked every fifteen minutes to see if they needed to use the restroom or other care. Now that you have heard the media spin, the actual truth is that all the alleged safety restraint chair victims were sought out by the prosecutors *to be* victims. None of them, other than Cleveland Jackson who was working on one of my political opponent's campaigns, ever made a complaint at the time or after they were authorized to be in the safety restraint chair and they never charged me with Cleveland Jackson because they knew it would make it obvious what the case was really about. Prosecutors only pulled the reports of the times I authorized the use of the safety restraint chair out of the 630 times it was used by my staff and contacted them to tell them they were victims and to have them testify. If the FBI contacts a criminal and tells them they are victims and can get their charges dropped and sue to get money, do you think it will be hard to convince a violent criminal to go along with that? So, we must ask and answer, how did all of this really get started?

Politically Motivated

The conflict between Clayton County DA, Tasha Mosley, and I date back to my first term in office as sheriff. As stated earlier, Mosley ran with a slate of my political enemies, including Kem Kimbrough who ran against me for sheriff back in 2008. Since then, she has always endorsed my political opponents, and the 2020 election was no exception. In this race, an ally of Mosley and a former deputy, Robert Hawes, who I fired and arrested ran against me for sheriff. This former deputy and his wife are friends with the Clayton County DA. I fired and arrested Robert Hawes for filing a false report concerning two missing firearms that were issued to him from the sheriff's office. He was also fired for falsifying a ticket for a stripper, issuing it to her as an alibi for staying out all night from her significant other. It was questionable why Hawes was even employed at the sheriff's office in the first place since he had been fired by the Atlanta Police Department for being out of the city at a woman's house in Clayton County while on duty instead of on patrol in the city of Atlanta.

Robert Hawes's wife, Gerrian Hawes, had to be arrested as well for repeatedly sending harassing messages to my email after her husband was fired. Both were arrested by me a couple of years before the politically motivated charges were brought against me. Ironically, but not surprisingly, neither one of them has gone to trial yet while my case has been adjudicated and I have now done most of my prison sentence. Mosley transferred their cases to other DA offices in other jurisdictions, with the intent to have their charges dismissed. Gerrian Hawes continues to run a magazine scam, calling it *South Atlanta Magazine*, to give the impression she is the southern branch of the legitimate *Atlanta Magazine*. Not too long after I arrested Hawes and his wife, Mosley called me on the phone one day to inform me Gerrian Hawes would be coming to the courthouse to interview her for a feature in her magazine and wanted her to be cleared to enter the courthouse. I asked Mosley if she thought it was a conflict of interest to be interviewed by a woman whom I had arrested along with her husband with the case being before her for prosecution. I also asked her if she realized the magazine, was a scam. You could tell she did not like what I said but canceled the interview.

One of Robert Hawes's campaign workers was a man named Cleveland Jackson. Cleveland Jackson was a man who had numerous run-ins with the sheriff's office prior to working on the Hawes's campaign, exhibiting violent and bizarre behavior. During the campaign, Jackson would come up to the sheriff's office with aggressive behavior, being disruptive while wearing "Hawes for Sheriff" campaign paraphernalia. He was already someone who previously had been in the safety restraint chair at least two times based on his violent behavior that clearly signaled pre-attack indicators for law enforcement and was placed in the restraint chair again.

Robert and Gerrian Hawes began posting on social media, complaining that Jackson had been put in the safety restraint chair because he was a supporter of theirs. Mosley, who was supporting the Hawes's campaign while working on getting the charges against them dropped, had her investigator Dennis Baker, who was attached to the FBI's taskforce, initiate an investigation to get the feds involved. Dennis Baker was also the lead investigator who previously coordinated my indictment as sheriff in 2012 with the felony RICO charges for driving my own patrol car out of town.

It was an easy sell to the feds to come after me. The local US attorneys and FBI agents are not very well known. They are also not allowed to have news cameras in the federal courthouse, which takes away from the TV time they all crave. The FBI and the US Attorney's Office are famous as an entity, the people who work there are not. They suffer immensely from the Robert Ford Syndrome, as much as local prosecutors and crave for fifteen seconds of fame just as much. They are starving for a big case to make a name for themselves to get on TV with a press conference too. But the problem they had was if they used Cleveland Jackson as the one and only complainant to get a search warrant to create a case against me, it would be obvious what this was about since he was front and center in the Hawes's campaign for sheriff. They needed someone else to make a complaint.

And thus entered Glen Howell, the landscaper.

To understand how the Glen Howell incident got to the feds, you must know who brought him to the table, and that was the locally elected sheriff of Butts County, Gary Long. Sheriff Long was a political enemy from the past. Long was a deputy investigator at the Clayton County sheriff's office in 2012, when former Sheriff Kimbrough coordinated with Tasha Mosley and Tracy Graham Lawson to indict me on RICO charges to stop me from running for reelection. Long won his election in Butts County at the same time I won back my seat in Clayton County. When Long became sheriff in Butts County, he took a lot of the Clayton County sheriff's employees with him who knew they could not work for me, including my former Assistant Chief Shaun Southerland who resigned under investigation for taking kickbacks from a carpet contractor he arranged to do work without going through the bidding process. Long is friends with DA Mosley, former DA Tracy Graham Lawson, and DA Investigator Dennis Baker, and knew what they were planning. And he just happened to be friends with Glen Howell, the landscaper. DA Dennis Baker was the lead investigator to indict me back in 2008. Now he was on the FBI task force leading this investigation on my use of the safety restraint chair.

"The Landscaper" Backstory

Prosecutors and the press portrayed Glen Howell as an innocent landscaper who was just trying to make a living and was not paid for work rendered to one of my deputies. They tried to make it appear as though I threatened him and told him my deputy did not have to pay him. They lied. Here is what happened:

I received a call from one of my Deputies, Joshua Guthrie, asking me if I had read the email he sent up the chain of command to me. I could tell by his voice he was distressed. The deputy explained to me that he had Howell doing some work on his property in Butts County and that they had a disagreement on how much money was to be exchanged. Guthrie described how Howell became danger-ously aggressive and destructive and that he believed Howell was on drugs. Guthrie went on to explain that Howell not only continuously made threats to him by phone and nasty remarks about him being in law enforcement, but also tore up his yard when he was not home and ran his girlfriend off the road in her car, with his vehicle. The deputy went on to tell me that this landscaper was repeatedly driving by his house and that he was not sure what to do. He thought the situation was going to end in a violent confrontation. I asked him if he had made a police report and he stated he had done so, but the police were not taking any real preventative actions to stop Howell's aggression, which appeared to only be getting worse. I told Guthrie to give me Howell's number and let me see if I could talk to him and calm the situation down.

I called Howell and told him who I was and that I would like to talk to him and that I was at my office and would love for him to stop by so he could know it was me and not a prank phone call.

"What is this about?" he asked.

"It is my understanding that you were having a dispute with one of my deputies over payment for services and I wanted to see if I could resolve it."

Howell told me my deputy owed him money and I replied, "That may well be the case. Why don't you come make a formal complaint with my internal affairs if you would like. I want to ex-plore any options other than a confrontation, where someone could get hurt."

Unprovoked, Howell became belligerent and began cursing and making threats toward me. Seeing that he was unable to reason with me, I politely hung up the phone. But it did not stop there. Howell kept calling via FaceTime and texting, continuously making threats. It was obvious that my deputy was correct in his assessment that Howell was dangerous and was not going to stop his aggressive behavior toward him or his family. I had my deputies file harassing communications warrants and sent my units out to look for him immediately to get him off the streets.

When my deputies got to Butts County, they called the Butts County sheriff's office for assistance. They explained who they were looking for and why and the deputies began assisting them. But then things took a bizarre turn. I got a call from the Butts County sheriff asking why we were looking for Howell when it was only a misdemeanor warrant. I explained to him the seriousness of this situation, how he had torn up the deputy's yard and ran his girlfriend off the road while making continuous threats and kept going by his house and was now continuing to call and make threats toward me as well. Usually, when you tell another elected sheriff something like this, he will send an army to help you, but that was not the case with Sheriff Long.

What I did not know at the time was that Sheriff Long was friends with Howell and that Howell's family were financial supporters of Long's campaign. Sheriff Long had a vested interest in protecting Howell despite the things he was doing to my deputy, his family, and myself. Glenn Howell ended up turning himself in three days later and was placed in the safety restraint chair for observation.

The safety restraint chair observation form clearly has a list of reasons to place individuals in the safety restraint chair for observation:

aggressive behavior, destructive behavior, and suicidal behavior. Based on his actions, he was placed in the safety restraint chair because of the serious pre-attack indicators he exhibited that clearly came under the aggressive and destructive behavior clause. I informed Howell that if he had a dispute with Guthrie over pay, to take him to court and pursue it that way and stop his aggressive and violent behavior. That was the end of it. Or at least, that is what I thought. Gary Long, who was already in cahoots with Clayton DA Tasha Mosley and her Lead Investigator Dennis Baker who was on the FBI task force, was waiting for a way to use my procedures for dealing with violent people against me. And that is exactly what they did.

It was approximately three weeks later that the FBI showed up at my office with a search warrant. I was in a crime statistics meeting when they arrived. When I asked what it was about, they were very tight-lipped, not wanting to say anything. They showed me a copy of the search warrant which only had two initials on it of two alleged victims. One of the agents asked me if I recognized the initials and I told him the only person I knew with those initials was a woman I had to arrest named Gerrian Hawes. The agent burst out laughing and stopped when the other agent looked at him in dismay. I asked the agent if he knew Gerrian Hawes and he replied, "Well, let's just say I've heard of her." It was a dead giveaway, and I knew he was lying. I also knew, at that moment, whatever this was about, Tasha Mosley—my longtime political enemy—was behind it and she was employing the feds to help her. After they obtained what they came to look for, they left.

The Investigation

After they left my office with the search warrant, their investigation began. Remember, we had never had any complaints about our use of the safety restraint chair until now and my staff had used it 623 times independently of me for the exact same reasons I did. But the FBI was not interested in that, they were only interested in the times I authorized used it so they could make a case against me. If they truly were interested in righting a new wrong they were now creating, they would have contacted all 630 people who were restrained in the chair and prosecuted every member of my staff that used the safety restraint chair to keep the jail safe as I did. They only investigated every case they could find where I was the one who authorized the use of the restraint chair. There was one case they pulled where they thought I had authorized its use, but when a lieutenant they interviewed told them he was the one who ordered the use of the chair, they were no longer interested. So, out of the total 630 times the safety restraint chair was authorized by members of my staff at all levels of rank, my use—and only my use—of the safety restraint chair became the subject of the federal criminal investigation and prosecution.

Indictment

I just got through speaking at a police officer's funeral when my lead attorney kept trying to call me on the phone. I excused myself and walked outside to see what he wanted, and he told me there was a sealed indictment from a federal grand jury on four counts of civil rights violations and that I needed to turn myself in.

The next day, I turned myself in at FBI headquarters, fully

compliant just like Raymond Reddington did in the first episode of *The Blacklist*. And guess what? The first thing they did was put me in restraints. Was it the safety restraint chair? No. But it was waist chains in leg shackles. I had no problems with it because I figured they had "prior knowledge" of me studying several different martial arts as well as being a trained sniper, so they were doing it just as a precaution to protect themselves, just like I did when I dealt with people, I knew were potentially violent. However, I did think it was comically hypocritical to charge me with using restraints for a person who turned himself in, with pre-attack indicators directed at one of my deputies and me as a preventative measure, when I had not shown them any pre-attack indicators by making threats against them.

Judge Assignment

Once we found out who the judge was assigned to my case, the incestuous relationships in my case became clearer. A friend of mine researched Judge Eleanor Ross and contacted me with concerns. First, her husband was an assistant prosecutor with the Clayton County DA's office at the time they attempted to prosecute me for allegedly violating the RICO act by driving my assigned vehicle out of town, and second, she also had a friendship with Tasha Mosley. Even more interesting was that she was Facebook friends with one of my longtime political opponents. This would later explain why, no matter what legal issues were about to be raised about the validity of the case, it would fall mute on deaf ears.

Ex-US Attorney Joins My Legal Team

As if a guardian angel was sent from above, an amazing lawyer jumped into the fight on my behalf. Attorney Lynsey Barron, who was a former prosecutor in the US Attorney's Office that was now prosecuting me, read the indictments against me and knew something was not right. She was able to get in contact with me and volunteered to represent me for free to assist in my legal representation.

The first thing that struck me was when Barron explained I was the first in the history of the United States to ever be charged with using the safety restraint chair and nothing more. She said, as far as she found from her research, no one had even been sued for so little. Barron went on to explain that the law forbids anyone from being prosecuted for a crime there was no clearly established law for. Baron explained that the irony, in this case, was that the US Attorney's Office was claiming they were trying to protect the civil rights of the inmates and were violating my civil rights by charging me with a crime of first impression. Baron stated the whole time she'd been in the US Attorney's Office, anytime a case came before them for prosecution regarding the use of the safety restraint chair, it was always the chair plus some type of violence while the person was restrained.

Lindsey Barron filed a motion to dismiss the indictment based on all of this. Ironically, at the time she filed this motion, two cases for the United States Supreme Court came out overturning two cases of use of force on the exact same premise. The problem was Baron didn't realize she was stepping into a political web of incestuous relationships. This judge was not going to dismiss the case, no matter what the case law stated. The plan was to allow it to go forward no matter what the law said, forcing me to take a plea.

Superseding Indictments

When I was first indicted, it was only a four-count indictment, and the government knew that their case was very weak, so they began looking to solicit more alleged victims to strengthen their case. When you look at who solicited two of the additional alleged restraint chair victims, it is very telling.

Tracy Graham-Lawson, the former DA who was the lead in the thirty-seven-count RICO indictment against me for driving my car out of town, was now in private practice with an attorney named Thomas Flournoy. Thomas Flournoy *just happened* to be the attorney representing Robert and Gerrian Hawes after I had them arrested. Flournoy *just happened* to have a client named Desmond Bailey, who told him he was in the safety restraint chair he referred to the FBI, which was added as a count. But what was interesting about Bailey was that he produced pictures that showed what looked like a deep cut on his wrist he said came from the cuffs in the safety restraint chair being too tight. Everyone who is placed in the safety restraint chair is checked by a nurse to make sure the cuffs are not too tight, and it is documented on a medical report. There is no way a nurse would clear anyone to be restrained with a cut on their wrist. It was obvious Bailey rocked his hands in the cuffs in order to be let out of the chair early for treatment which he was.

Another alleged safety restraint victim produced for another count was Walter Thomas. Walter Thomas was a textbook example of how prosecutors are allowed to lie to a grand jury with impunity. The indictment on Walter Thomas said that a mask was placed over his head while several officers and I were standing there, and then he was punched in the face. However, no suspect was named or indicted for doing so not once during my trial. After reviewing FBI reports, it was revealed who solicited Walter Thomas to be an alleged restraint chair victim. Walter Thomas admitted he was a friend of Robert Hawes, the deputy I had fired and arrested. Also, as unbelievable as it sounds, Walter Thomas said Jonathan Newton, the man who had to resign years ago for taking kickbacks from the sheriff's office and believed to fake a bachelor's degree to get into law school to become an attorney, was representing him. It was clear the whole crew of people I had fired and arrested over the years were working with the Clayton County DA Tasha Mosley to pile up as many counts as they could to make it stick or get me to take a plea so that they could get their charges dropped and their jobs back. Also, we must note that Chairman Jeff Turner is friends with DA Tasha Mosley and still wanted me out of the way so he could run for sheriff. Turner tried to get the Governor to appoint him sheriff after my suspension that followed my indictment. These facts of how this case came to be is something the jury should have been made aware of. However, as you will see, the prosecutors and judge made sure they would prevent the jury from hearing any of these crucial facts so they could get a conviction.

Chapter 12

Federal Trial

I never thought it would be possible to liken a federal trial to a kangaroo court, but my trial would prove to be as such with more hopping around than actual kangaroos. I was already the first in the country to be prosecuted for authorizing the use of the restraint chair only, but what the judge would allow to happen and say during this trial would not only be a first as well, but would become the subject of my appeal to the Eleventh Circuit Court of Appeals for actions that have never been seen or heard of before in a federal trial.

Selective Prosecution

To show my case was one of selective prosecution, we need not look any further than Gwinnett County, Georgia. The Gwinnett County Jail had a well-publicized lawsuit concerning the use of the restraint chair where Gwinnett County deputies rushed into jail cells and assaulted non-resisting, compliant inmates, prior to placing them into a restraint chair. The justice department did an investigation, and miraculously no one was criminally charged. There were other cases across the country even worse than the Gwinnett County case, where the justice department did not criminally charge anyone, even though the inmates in some of these cases actually died in the safety restraint chair. (See appendix) Prosecutors filed a motion to make sure we could not use these comparisons or anything that would make their prosecution of me suspicious of political motivation. Presiding Judge Eleanor Ross granted the prosecutors every advantage in this motion to limit us using these facts in my defense.

Mock Jury

Prior to going to trial, I wanted to do everything I could to prepare. It was extremely important for me to have an assessment of how a jury would view the facts of my case. Therefore, I insisted that my attorneys employ a mock jury. A mock jury is when you employ people to sit and act as jurors while presenting proposed evidence from the prosecution and defense to get their unbiased opinion of why they would vote guilty or not guilty. When we did this, the mock jury we hired was unable to reach a unanimous verdict. When the jurors who stated they could not vote guilty were asked why, all of them gave the same answer. They said that whether they agreed with my use of the safety restraint chair or not, if policy and law gave me the authority to use the chair in that manner, then I was not guilty of a crime. They reasoned that if I did not have the intent to violate a law based on training and policy, I was not guilty of a crime.

Cleveland Jackson Shows up Every Day for Trial

Cleveland Jackson, the campaign worker for Robert Hawes, the deputy I fired and arrested, showed up at the trial, faithfully, every day, and constantly acted out in the hallway to the point that security needed to be called on him several times. It was obvious the FBI were afraid of him and some of my friends thought maybe this would get them to see the value of the safety restraint chair when dealing with unstable violent individuals like him. Cleveland even approached my lead attorney in the bathroom in an aggressive manner. We had a witness that Cleveland Jackson said he was working with the FBI to get me out of office so he could get his guy in office. However, as stated, we were not allowed to present background of how this case came to be before the jury, and interestingly, the judge would not allow the victims of the men I restrained in the chair for safety to testify on just how violent and crazy they were. All of this of course was by design to coerce a guilty verdict.

Jury Selection

Jury selection was very interesting from day one. The government was very careful to make sure no one from Clayton County got on the jury. They knew the people from Clayton County knew me and my work and we're very aware of the politics that had gone over a decade to try to get me removed from office. They were looking for people who didn't stay close to Clayton County and only watched the one-sided news clips the media would do to influence a jury for a guilty verdict. But there were still some in the jury pool who found the case to be highly suspicious. One possible jury member asked the court if he could ask a question and when the court allowed it, he asked why the FBI would be involved in a case like this. Of course, he was struck from being on the jury. Once the jury was selected, another jury member came in the first day before trial and said he couldn't sleep and couldn't eat because he couldn't see himself sending me to jail for doing my job. Of course, the judge gladly struck him from the jury and he was replaced.

The Government's Witnesses

The government never presented how the case came to be and due to what the judge limited us to, we were not allowed to present these facts either. Almost every witness was someone that I had fired or arrested, if not both. Witness after witness came in of people I had arrested, fired, or demoted, and many were employees that resigned in lieu of investigation that were not prosecuted by the DA Mosley for stealing $1.5 million in overtime. All of them gave their opinion that they disagreed with my use of the restraint chair. If the government had looked at the other 623 times the chair was employed, it was done by some of their witnesses against me under similar circumstances. All of them should have been cross-examined if the policy said the chair could be used for preventive purposes and if annual state training supported by case law trained them that "prior knowledge" of a person's propensity for violence allows preemptive use of force as well as passive restraints. But they were not, and that is another story for another time.

The Secret Recording Whistleblower

A former deputy, Hannah James—who resigned from the sheriff's office after being removed from the fugitive squad and SWAT team for being at a party in her assigned police vehicle while drinking , claiming she could not come to work when a five-year-old was shot because she had too much to drink—gave prosecutors a video she was holding for over a year. James claimed she was so disturbed by inmates going into the restraint chair, she recorded it to give to the government. If this was the case, why did she hold on to the video and not show it to anyone for over a year? The truth was Hannah James recorded the video to brag to her friends that she had a hand in catching the man who had savagely beaten a mother and grandmother in a grocery store. If you look at the video where "the landscaper" was restrained, you can see her running to put him in the restraint chair as if she was happy to do it, even though she is not a jail officer.

Comically, after the trial, she did a TV interview with reporters hiding her face as if her life was in danger. Maybe she did not want anyone to recognize her as strapping "the landscaper" in the safety restraint chair when that video aired. As I have stated before, all of the witnesses in my trial were either people I fired or arrested if not both, with a motive to lie to help prosecutors get a conviction. Many of them, like James, were those who had placed others in the restraint chair the 623 time the chair was used absent of my authorization. If this truly is a crime, why would prosecutors give them a free pass to violate inmates' rights and why weren't these inmates contacted to be told they were victims so they could get their charges dropped and offered settlements?

Urination of Lies

All of my so-called victims claimed they urinated on themselves. This lie was just another example of how prosecutors would coach people to lie on the stand to get a conviction. Let's think about this for a minute. If they had urinated on themselves, where were the decontamination reports of the safety restraint chair being disinfected after it was soaked in urine? Where was the report of these inmates having to be issued fresh uniforms and allowed to shower? Even better, when they were checked on every fifteen minutes while restrained in the chair, were they told they could not use the restroom from the officers who would be responsible for cleaning up the urine? If these officers really did refuse to allow these seven inmates the right to use the restroom, why did the prosecutors not prosecute them for torturing inmates to sit in their own urine? Would that not be a violation of their civil rights? It's amazing how witnesses are coached and allowed to lie on the stand without recourse of perjury for them or the prosecutors who coach them to lie.

My Testimony

I knew I was going to testify in trial. Most defendants don't, but I knew the jury needed to hear from me. The main issue I wanted to hammer in was that the annual state training all peace officers received teaches that we have the option to use restraints preemptively if we have prior knowledge of the potential for violence of the individual. Personnel at the jail had pulled records confirming that after my suspension and the halt of the use of the restraint chair for fear of political prosecution, assaults went up on officers by over 100 percent and inmate-on-inmate assaults went up by over 200 percent, as well as two people getting killed in the jail by the time of my trial which was unheard of prior to this novel prosecution. My testimony was able to get most of these facts in but should have been corroborated by the witnesses that were not allowed to testify such as the victims of the inmates I authorized to be restrained. It was my testimony that caused the jury to deliberate for four days, unable to come up with a unanimous verdict.

But despite all these facts, I testified to the jury being deadlocked for four days, Judge Ross would do everything in her power to coerce a guilty verdict. The foreman of the jury began sending a series of inflammatory notes, singling out a juror because he would not vote to convict me. The forewoman began accusing the juror of everything possible to get the judge to remove the juror.

Judge Ross called out this juror in front of everyone including the press, to inquire if he was cognitively impaired based on the forewoman's notes. It turned out he was not, and articulated how he was considering "the willful intent" part of the law I was being charged with. The juror also described how he was being yelled at and called names by his fellow jurors. This alone should have caused the judge to declare a mistrial, but she would do nothing of the sort. Judge Ross was visibly upset at the possibility of having to declare a mistrial. This would become even more obvious when she did something never seen in the Eleventh Circuit or any other circuit.

Perhaps the craziest thing in my trial was when Judge Ross began speaking directly to the media sitting in the audience after bringing out the juror, who was identified in front of the world as the holdout juror. She told them she knew they wanted this juror kicked off but that she could not find a lawful reason to do so at the time. Judge Ross knew the press wanted my head and was trying to assure them that she was working diligently to give it to them. The media has untold perceived power over elected and appointed officials who want to be praised by them on the six o'clock news, hoping to build a name for themselves.

Her actions got even more bizarre when she called the juror out again for a second time, to question him *again* in front of the press before sending him back into a situation the holdout juror had already described as volatile because of the jurors who were yelling at him and calling him names. There is no record of this ever being done before and was unprecedented. Judge Ross had too much invested in this case to please her friends and the media, who were counting on her to get a conviction.

On the final day of deliberation, Lynsey Barron, my volunteer, pro-bono attorney, found a case in the Eleventh Circuit that was almost identical to what was happening in my trial where the judge knew the jury split and allowed the trial to go forward without declaring a mistrial. Judge Ross acted as if she was not aware of the motion sent by email, and disregarded it, determined to coerce a verdict.

Judge Ross was unable to hide her personal bias and feelings in this case. When Ross insisted on charging the jury a second time, she misread the charge at the part where it said, "If there's any reasonable doubt, I should be found *not guilty*," and instead said, "I should be found *guilty*." I will never forget the emphasis she put on the word "guilty" when she misread the charge to the jury.

Guilty on Six Out of Seven Counts

After being yelled at, berated, and called names by his fellow jurors, and coerced by Judge Ross to be called out in front of the public and the press twice, the man identified by the media as the "holdout juror" finally gave into the pressure and went along with convicting me on six out of seven counts. What was amazing was that the only count I was not convicted on was the one incident where it was clearly on film that I was not the person who authorized to put the alleged victim in the safety restraint chair. It was clearly one of my Sergeants who authorized the use of the safety restraint chair in the video, and I wasn't even there.

Here is the magic question: If the US prosecutors and the judge thought that none of the seven should have been placed in a safety restraint chair, why is it that they did not pursue charges against the sergeant for violating that inmate's constitutional rights? Was it only illegal for him to be placed in the safety restraint chair if I authorized it? This was further proof that the case was targeted to me and me only. I was tried and wrongfully convicted for a crime no one in law enforcement ever knew existed—because it did not exist. If this happened to me, how many others has it already happened to that are sitting in prison, as I now do, who did not have the means to fight or the voice to be heard? I believe the numbers are more staggering than we can imagine.

After my conviction, one of the videos shown in court of me addressing an inmate before he was placed into the safety restraint chair was released to the media and played on every news channel. It showed me telling the inmate he sounded like a jackass. He did. It also showed me responding to one of his statements that he has rights, replying, "Not in my county." Even though it should be obvious that I was making it clear he did not have the right to beat up old ladies, it was spun, of course, to make it look like I meant he had no constitutional rights.

Later, while in jail, other officers had to place him back in the safety restraint chair again for striking another inmate with a food tray. It should not be a surprise that the tape of him savagely beating a sixty-year-old mother and an eighty-year-old grandmother in an electric wheelchair for allegedly cutting in front of him in line was not shown at my trial. It is also interesting that the media who aired that footage as an outrage, stopped airing it after I was indicted for violating his constitutional rights.

The mother and grandmother in this case wanted to testify for me but were not allowed to, as with all of the other victims of the violent individuals I authorized to be restrained. This main example, out of the seven inmates, shows how media and prosecutors have and continue to make victims out of violent criminals and villainize those who protect society from them if it serves their purpose. What did the prosecutors and media accomplish with this victory of convicting me and dropping the charges on these individuals as well as giving them settlements? If all they cared about was getting me out of office and getting back at me for ignoring them, their objective was met, but at what cost?

Since all of this has occurred, four inmates have been murdered at the jail, and one trying to commit suicide was accidentally smothered to death by officers holding him down, afraid to use the restraint chair. Stabbings of inmates and assault on officers are now commonplace at the Clayton County Jail. The inmate population they claimed they were protecting from *me*, are now in grave danger every day, and some must even get their family members to pay violent inmates "protection money" via Cash App. This move by prosecutors and press gave violent criminals a win they are enjoying to the fullest at the expense of their victims—not just in the jail, but even in the streets of Clayton County. After my indictment, law enforcement in Clayton County began handling violent criminals with kid gloves and the murder rate rose to an all-time high. I often wonder if these prosecutors and press members would be so endearing and concerned for the protection of violent criminals from the likes of me if it was their mother or grandmother savagely beaten in a grocery store.

My political enemies may have, after a decade of trying, finally got me, but was it worth it for all the victims who have been stabbed and the four who were killed at the jail? Did the fifteen seconds of fame propel them to national prominence for defending the constitutional rights of the violent criminals they claim was their only and pure objective? It appears not, but the objective of our local DA is still possible if her friend Jeff Turner is elected sheriff since removing me from office was his only hope to get the seat of which he has announced he is now a candidate for sheriff since my false imprisonment.

After my conviction, while waiting to receive my sentence, something else happened no one saw coming that would shed much more light and connect the dots on the involvement of DA Tasha Mosley and Chairman Jeff Turner in the plot to have me criminally charged and indicted to get me out of office. Information from an inside source among their ranks.

Chairman Turner's Executive Assistant Arrested

On January 24, 2023, Katrina Holloway, the Executive Assistant to Chairman Jeff Turner was arrested by the GBI for allegedly sending threatening letters written to imply the letters came from me to threaten Jeff Turner. They made this arrest solely on the fact that the stamps on the letters were bought with her debit card. After Holloway was arrested and posted bond, she immediately began to tell her story, further confirming what we knew to be true. Holloway stated Jeff Turner had come to her office and asked her for a couple of stamps to mail some letters off. Miss Holloway stated she gave the stamps to him, having no idea he was staging a fake threat letter to himself. Now, because of a mistake he made by using her stamps, he was allowing her to take the fall for a crime he committed and fired her to cover his tail. The letter was written in a way to imply they came from me. Turner was trying to find a way to get my bond revoked before I went to trial because he felt I had influence on three board members who had voted to strip him of most of his powers as Chairman. Furthermore, there is no reason for Katrina Holloway to fake a letter implying I was threatening Jeff Turner. I have known the Holloway family through a great relationship with her father for decades, so there would be no motive for Katrina Holloway to want my bond revoked or have me imprisoned early. However, there was a motive because Turner would want me not able to run for office and not around. Not only did he attempt to run for sheriff in 2012, having to withdraw and run for chairman due to qualification issues, but as stated, he has announced he is now running for sheriff while I am now incarcerated.

After Holloway's arrest, she stated that Clayton County DA Tasha Mosley sent two women, Ramona Bivins and Chalanda Smith who are both friends to the DA and Turner and former county employees to meet with her at The French Market and

Tavern in Locust Grove, Georgia. According to Holloway, both women told her that the DA wanted her to claim insanity and say she was under emotional duress because she was afraid of me. The two women said the DA also wanted her to say that not only did she fear for her life, but she was also fearful for the life of the DA, Tasha Mosley and Turner. They both suggested to her that she use the insurance she still had time left on, since she had just been fired, to go seek mental health treatment—that way she could use it as part of her defense when it went to court so that DA Tasha Mosley could use this to eventually drop the charges, leaving Jeff Turner to look innocent. They even gave her an attorney to contact to help move this coverup along. Holloway stated she became incensed at the whole idea because she had nothing to do with writing the fake letter written by Turner. Holloway told the two women she was not going to lie to protect Turner and take the fall for what he did. Holloway then surprised them and went public with her story. She also revealed more details about the Clayton County DA's involvement in my case.

It is important to know that Katrina Holloway is related to the Clayton County DA. They are third cousins. This makes the information Katrina Holloway gave, as an addition to what happened with her arrest, far more insightful and shows how insidious the whole situation really was. It also gives further credibility that the sitting DA felt comfortable engaging in gossip with her about what she knew and was involved with behind the scenes. Holloway, working for Turner who was friends with her cousin the DA, was privy to a lot of conversations—more than most executive assistants. Most telling were her accounts of Chairman Turner making frequent attempts to contact the governor, hoping he would suggest appointing him sheriff.

Holloway also stated that anytime I would terminate an employee, Jeff Turner would meet with them and encourage them to file a lawsuit, making recommendations of attorneys for them to go see. Notably, Holloway recalled Hannah James, the so-called whistleblower who hid her face on TV, coming to meet with Turner after she resigned for being disciplined for drinking while in a county vehicle. Holloway said Turner would tell all of the employees I had to terminate that he would help them win what he referred to as the "Clayco lottery." After they would sue, Turner would begin publicly campaigning, telling anyone who would listen that I was costing the county money while he was the one encouraging and coordinating the lawsuits promising them his help. Holloway said she always felt that it was sad the chairman who was responsible for guarding the county's coffers was trying to give it away as a part of a plot to see if it could get him elected sheriff. Turner's actions not only cost the county money in unnecessary lawsuits he encouraged, but now that the plot he and DA Tasha Mosley contrived to get him elected sheriff has resulted in five inmates being killed in the jail, the county will pay an astronomical amount of money for wrongful death suits.

If there was any doubt about Holloway's information, the fact that Jeff Turner is now running for sheriff should remove any doubt about his involvement in this plot with DA Tasha Mosley. Holloway stated that during her time as Jeff Turner's administrative assistant, she had various conversations with Tasha Mosley about my case. Holloway stated, one day, Tasha Mosley asked her to call the

Federal Probation Office to see if she could get my bond revoked. This happened just before Turner staged the letter to himself, trying to see if he could make the GBI think the letter came from me to get my bond revoked. Holloway stated Mosley said she needed someone else to call them and say something, to see if they could revoke my bond to get me off of the streets so I could not affect the politics on the board. Holloway declined to make the call. Holloway also stated that Tasha told her she knew Judge Ross and her husband, who used to work at the Clayton County DA's Office and felt confident Judge Ross would work diligently to make sure I got convicted. This was consistent with another source who told me the judge's husband had a friendly relationship with Jeff Turner. Holloway also stated Mosley told her that once I was convicted, she was hopeful Judge Ross would give me enough time where I would be gone and not involved in the politics of Clayton County for a long time to come. Most disturbing was when Holloway said that during the time of my trial, when there was a holdout juror, Tasha told her "they" were reaching out to the family of the holdout juror to influence him to vote guilty in my case.

Holloway also provided information on Chairman Turner having illegal dealings with nonprofits, of which she observed him receiving kickbacks. She also had information about his involvement with a shady company called Roman United that claimed they were going to bring a billion-dollar development to Clayton County. Jeff Turner had arranged for them to get over half a million dollars for the project that was never started and was never going to get started.

As good as all this information was, the problem for Holloway was that the DA was personal friends with Turner—to the point she wanted Holloway to take the fall for Turner, despite them being blood relatives.

Katrina Hollaway would also give insight into actions of the Clayton County DA that were even more sinister than conjuring charges to come after political opponents—Tasha Mosley's cover-up of the child molestation cases at the Rainbow House.

The Rainbow House

The Rainbow House is one of the biggest travesties that has ever occurred in Clayton County. It would reveal just how corrupt the Clayton County DA is when it comes to covering up crimes committed by her friends, even at the expense of children being violated. Tasha Mosley, as a political move, got herself placed on the board of directors for the nonprofit Rainbow House. This facility was designed to provide care for children displaced from their homes after sexual abuse while going through the court system. It was supposed to be a haven for those children to receive the help they needed. Instead of being a haven, it was a haven for the largest sexual abuse cover-up under the leadership of Mosley.

It was reported a staff member who was supposed to be keeping these children—already dealing with the aftereffects of abuse—was a pedophile himself. It was the son of the director of Rainbow House, who was hired and managed by DA Mosley and Rainbow House Board members, who sexually abused several of the children repeatedly. The son of the director was fired, and then, remarkably, rehired under the direction and leadership of Tasha Mosley.

Holloway reported that when she was working for Jeff Turner, the first complaint about this came from a whistleblower employee about what was happening at the Rainbow House, and she put this complaint on his desk. Later, she saw the complaint in his trash can.

Despite Hollway putting out this information, it fell on deaf ears. The DA, who is supposed to be investigating these matters, was involved and was not going to look into herself or her friends. This is the fallacy of how the system fails when you have the head prosecutor of the county involved in incidents like this and there is no check and balance process in place to hold these types of prosecutors accountable. So far, nothing has been done about Tasha Mosley or Jeff Turner for not reporting or taking the necessary action when this case was first brought to their attention. Also, nothing has been done about DA Mosley allowing the son of the director to be rehired—after he was fired—and sexually abused more children.

Sentencing

March 14, 2023, was the date for my sentencing. When I arrived, the parking lot was full of reporters as usual. Nothing had changed my policy of ignoring the media and this was my last appearance at court to enjoy doing so. My brother had flown in to be present with me. We resemble each other, so the press focused the cameras on him not knowing it wasn't me. That was hilarious.

I already knew the judge was going to put on a show for the media so she could get the fifteen seconds of fame she fought so hard for by coercing a verdict. Plus, I knew she was mad about me continuing to influence the sheriff's race to throw a monkey wrench in their plot to get me out to get their man in so it was possible she was likely to retaliate by giving me more time. But I would have never guessed in a million years she would admit this on the record.

Before I directly quote what Judge Ross said to me from the court transcripts just before she sentenced me to eighteen months in prison, let me quote the code of conduct for all United States judges. The code of conduct says, "Judges may not hear cases in which they have either personal knowledge of the disputed facts, a personal bias concerning a party to the case, earlier involvement in the case as a lawyer, or a financial interest in any party or subject matter of the case." Think about this code of ethics as I quote directly from the court transcripts what Judge Ross said during my sentence hearing.

Judge Ross said,

> *The convictions for what we are dealing with in this case are pretty novel. I don't know if any of us have seen a prosecution, let alone a conviction, related to the use of a restraint chair. And in fact, I am not aware of any civil lawsuits on that basis either except for the ones now pending on Mr. Hill.*

It's truly amazing the judge came right out and admitted this was a novel case of first impression and she was not aware of any case law that said what I did was wrong. We must then ask, if this was the result of her legal research, why did she not dismiss the case when this fact was brought to her attention in a motion to dismiss filed by Attorney Barron? Her statement confirmed very clearly that it was a case that should have never gone before a jury according to case law, but it did, and it was forced through by jury coercion.

> *I have also considered that this type of prosecution is in this course estimation, novel, at best, and that this type of charge does often involve violence, assault of behavior, such as beating, tasing, shooting, etc., or unlawful arrest—none of which is involved here.*

Most of the time, when cops are charged with felony color of law cases, we see it in cases like Briana Taylor and George Floyd. I never touched, injured, or killed anyone, as in those cases. The statute states if there is no serious injury it is a misdemeanor. However, they needed a felony conviction to remove me from office and successfully ham-sandwich it through the grand jury process. Ross insisted on sending me to prison to please the press and her political friends.

> *Let me start by saying that I have truly struggled with this case. There has been a lot of thought, and contemplation, and because of the woman I am, I did a lot of prayer in this case, not because it is high profile.*

I'm a praying man too, but what happened to the separation of church and state? Also, if the case being high profile was not an issue, why bring it up?

I struggled with this case because, as we have already discussed, it is such a novel one.

This was another Freudian slip because, as we discussed, if she knew it was a novel case that had never been prosecuted before, why did she allow the case to go forward knowing it was a case of first impression with no case law to support that what I did was a crime?

And one thing I've come to realize, especially over the past year or so, is that everybody has a Victor Hill opinion.

Based on the facts that Judge Ross is Facebook friends with one of my political opponents, and friends with the Clayton County DA who brought this case to the US attorney, she obviously already had "a Victor Hill opinion" as well.

I've had to shut people down. Many people who know I am assigned to this case wanted to come talk about Victor Hill. And I've had to say, "No, it's not appropriate. I can't talk to you; I don't want to hear your opinion."

But it seems like those opinions are always at one extreme or another. You are either a hero or a villain to many people. There really is not any gray area when it comes to that.

I must ask and wonder how did she get to know I'm either a hero or villain to so many people if she shut them down, telling them no because listening to them is inappropriate?

But what I say today to everyone who has an interest at all in this case is that, although I can generally consider some character evidence, I am not here to punish Victor Hill for everything he's done.

Everything I have done? What exactly is *everything* I have done? Did the judge just assume I am guilty of everything anyone has ever accused me of?

People have sent me letters about all the people he terminated from the sheriff's office. I got a flash drive of the 911 call involving a woman and the shooting in Gwinnett County. I'm not here for any of that stuff.

Why did Judge Ross bring up "any of that stuff" if it had nothing to do with her decision? The fact she brought up "any of that stuff" made it obvious she was there for all of "that stuff." Who gave her a flash drive and how did they get it to her?

I don't mind telling you that based on your trial testimony and also, even though it's not a part of this record, some of your social media activity that I've seen since you got convicted, I'm not sure whether or not you've learned your lesson fully in this case. I know you are keeping your hands involved in the selection of the next sheriff.

Why was Judge Ross reading my social media? If it is not a part of the record, why was it a part of my sentencing? What offended her about it? Was it my support of another candidate she did not approve?

Then came this added measure to my probation from the judge and I quote,

> Additionally, and I need you to understand this clearly, pursuant to 18 U.S.C. Section 3653 (B) (5), you must refrain from engaging in the occupation business or professional law enforcement, including as a consultant. That means that if the next sheriff of Clayton County is someone closely associated with you, hypothetically, who wants to offer you a position as a civilian to circumvent your lack of post-certification, you would not be able to accept it. You will not be permitted to work in that capacity.
>
> And like you, I know many people; I have big ears. I will bring you into this courtroom and hold a supervised release hearing for this court to determine whether you've been working in such a law enforcement capacity.

Who said I had big ears? Was it the people she said she couldn't talk to? Also, does the many people she knows include the DA Tasha Mosley and Chairman Jeff Turner, who has announced he is running for sheriff after my wrongful conviction?

Hal's Steakhouse

The unprofessional statements and behavior of Judge Ross did not end at the sentencing. After sentencing that evening, I went to have dinner with my best friend at Hal's Steakhouse. When we walked in, we were seated upstairs and joined by a couple of attorneys who flew in from New York to weigh in on my appeal.

When we sat down at the table, within three to four minutes, I saw the silhouette of a woman walking up to the table in my peripheral vision. I immediately stood up to greet the lady to see who she was and what she wanted. To my surprise, and the surprise of everyone seated at my table, it was Judge Ross. She said she just wanted to come over and say hi, giving me a smug smile, and left.

Most judges would not approach anyone they had just sentenced earlier that day in a public setting—not just for security reasons, but ethically and professionally it is an odd position for both the judge and the person they sentenced. What if I wanted to express my disdain for her unethical behavior and connections to my political enemies? It was very inappropriate, to say the least, and I don't know any judge who would think her coming up to my table after sentencing me was a good idea. A kangaroo court indeed.

Monkey Wrench

I had a couple of months before I had to turn myself into federal prison. The special election for sheriff took place right before I had to leave. At the time, I wanted to throw a monkey wrench into the political plot Tasha Mosley and Jeff Turner had come up with to get me indicted and out of office so they could take control of the sheriff's office. So, I supported a candidate that was unknown, who most thought would not stand a chance in hell of winning. He won. All of that planning and plotting and they still did not achieve their ultimate objective. I smiled all the way to prison on a private jet.

Chapter 13

Forest City Federal Prison (M-B The Lion's Den)

T he Bible, in the book of Daniel, Chapter 6 says that when political officials wanted Daniel removed from office, they decided to charge him with a crime. In verses four through five it essentially reads that when these officials could not find a charge with which to prosecute Daniel, they got creative and came up with a novel prosecution. After coercing a conviction, Daniel was cast into a lion's den to be devoured.

It was May 15, 2023, when I turned myself into federal prison. I had to be there no later than twelve p.m. on this date. I had already arranged to take a flight on a private jet because the prison I was being sent to was in Forest City, Arkansas, a thousand miles away from Atlanta. A thousand miles is not the type of trip you wake up early in the morning to get there on time.

Once I arrived, I walked in through the front door and showed my ID to let them know I was there on time. Once I was booked in, I was told to report to the M-B unit and see the head orderly for my cell assignment. I was pointed in the direction of an open courtyard where there were three separate housing unit build-ings. The building I was assigned to was in the middle of the three housing unit buildings. Each building consisted of two separate housing units upstairs and downstairs. To the right of the central courtyard was the cafeteria and to the left, the recreation building and yard.

As I walked across the open courtyard, I was amazed at the amount of cats roaming freely across the complex, mostly hang-ing out by the cafeteria to get fed. I smiled because I love cats. They are entertaining to watch and wherever they are, there are no rodents because they kill them on site.

Though it was recommended I be sent to a camp as is commonly done with elected officials, I instead was sent to a so called "low security" federal prison in Forest City, Arkansas, and assigned to the worst housing unit on the compound with the most violent and unruly inmates. In housing unit M-B, inmates who were unwanted were told to go "check themselves in" to solitary confinement—better known there as "the chute." If unwanted inmates do not voluntarily do so, they are beaten mercilessly and forced to go to the guards to get themselves "checked in." Because of this, and what you are about to read, the M-B housing unit became known as "the lion's den" of the Forest City low-security federal prison.

Once I walked into the unit, you could cut the air with a knife. Everyone was already aware of who I was and my mode of trans-portation to get there. The majority were not happy. No one wanted a cop assigned to their unit. I asked who was the head orderly for the unit and was told his name was Wild Wild and where to find him. I remember wondering how he got a nickname like that. When

I saw him, I asked for a bunk assignment and he gave me one with no fanfare, but I could tell he was very observant and suspicious of me. Wild Wild, as I would later find out, not only ran the M-B unit, but he was a very high-ranking, five-star member of the Vice Lords. He was very well respected and feared across the compound. The cellmate Wild Wild assigned me to was a man who could be an identical twin to the rapper Rick Ross. He was polite and explained to me how the bathrooms were full of black mold, and that it had to be sprayed with disinfectant before use. He told me he had caught an infection twice from the restrooms so advised me to use caution, and he left. He was not exaggerating. The restrooms were one of the nastiest I had ever seen and constantly had leaks from the ceiling from the restroom above and plumbing leaks on the ground leaving large puddles of water in the middle walk area. At one point, the water began to leak over to the floors of the cells next to the restrooms.

Twenty minutes later, a young inmate came and told me I was being moved. He told me my cellmate went to Wild Wild after finding out I was a cop and told him he would prefer not to be cellmates with me. The young inmate said his family was from Atlanta and he knew of me. He asked me to come to a room so we could speak further in private. After we sat down, he told me everyone was concerned about having a cop in the unit and went further to say, "we got a lot going on in here," and did not need anyone snitching them out to the guards. My reply made him laugh. I asked him if he really thought the people who put me here were going to warm up to me and let me out early if I started giving them information on inmates. I then told him my sole objective was to do my time and leave, and as long as no one messed with me, I had no interest in messing with them. He respected my reply, we shook hands, and I returned to my new cell assignment.

Word was spreading fast across the complex of my arrival, which caused the head orderly from upstairs to come down and introduce himself to me. He introduced himself to me as ATL, which was his nickname since he was from Atlanta. ATL said he wanted to lay eyes on me to see if it was true I was here. I could tell he had authority, and his presence was respected, just like Wild Wild. I would later find out he was a drug lord in one of the metro Atlanta counties adjacent to mine. I did not know it at that moment, but ATL and I would develop a dialogue that would become one of the seeds that gave birth to this book.

Chess Not Checkers

Playing chess in prison was something I had anticipated and was looking forward to since I knew chess was a prison pastime and I expected to encounter some very high-level chess players. After my sentencing, I had contacted a well-known chess master in Atlanta, Orrin "Checkmate" Hudson, to arrange private lessons so that I could dominate the prison chess arena I was about to enter. Orrin and I were not able to get together, but he did give me some tips across the phone to help arm me as much as he could. The phone tips were not enough for what I was going to encounter.

After getting settled into my cell, I walked around to get familiar with my surroundings. I went inside a room where everyone was playing chess. There was not a checkers board in sight. What was interesting was that almost everyone in the room looked and acted like street thugs playing the game. There was a lot of cursing and calling players out as they referred to the pieces on the board in very derogatory terms. The queen was referred to as "the bitch." This was not the refined environment in which I was taught the game of chess. I thought, surely these thugs would not be a match for an experienced warlord. I got in line to play the winner.

It was a very humbling moment when I realized just how good these guys actually were and had to admit to myself, I was nowhere close to their level. I remember asking one of them how he got so good at chess. His reply astonished me. He said he had been in prison for nineteen years and had played the game almost every day of his sentence. I was in the presence of chess masters, and from that day on I became their student. I did not realize it then, but that moment was just the beginning of my "higher education" at the "Federal Forest City University." I could not forsee that I was going to eventually run into another group of chess-playing inmates who were playing on another level I had never seen or imagined. These guys were playing "four-dimensional chess," where four players play at the same time with each player having the sixteen-piece army on a board almost five times the size of a standard chess board. They played as two-man teams with the objective of checkmating either of the two individuals playing against them first for a win. Sometimes they played a ruthless no-team, every-man-for-himself game. This exclusive group of players would eventually let me into their fold to teach and allow me to play with them.

Two hours later, while still in the "chess room," I was summoned back to Receiving and Delivery (R&D) where I entered the prison by the Shift Lieutenant. He asked me if anyone was giving me any problems.

"Not at all," I replied.

The Lieutenant then asked if the inmates were aware of who I was. I replied, "Yes, they all are aware. I guess they have access to the internet."

He laughed and asked, "Are you scared?"

"Trust me, I'll be just fine," I replied.

The Lieutenant then said, "Well, if you have any problems, let me know."

I had spent the majority of my life around killers, so being locked up with them was really not a concern to me. My only real concern was that I did not want anyone to force me into a self-defense situation, causing me to get an unwanted murder charge to fight in addition to the political charges I'm appealing.

But who I was about to encounter on my way back to my unit did make me concerned for my safety. I was getting ready to meet a real gangster who did not give a you-know-what about me or anyone on the prison compound. If there was anyone to be afraid of, it was him. He and his gang ran everything on the yard, and everyone knew it.

Pepé Le Pew

As I was walking back to my assigned building, I saw a creature with a hump on his back walk around the other side of the trash can. It was a slow, relaxed, and confident stroll. I remember wondering how could a rat that large survive here with all of the cats I saw upon my arrival? I looked around to see where the nearest cat was because this was the fight I wanted to see. I saw a cat, but it was obvious he was not going to get involved. When what I thought was a rat emerged on the other side of the trash can, I realized it was a skunk. I had never actually seen a skunk in real life until this moment. I had only seen them on wildlife shows, and of course, the cartoon character and perhaps one of the greatest lovers of all times, Pepé Le Pew.

When he came around the other side of the trash can, we locked eyes. One of the rules of survival on the streets is to never break eye contact by looking down or away from your aggressor. It shows weakness. You make him blink and take his heart before you take him down. The skunk did not blink, and I walked away, immediately breaking eye contact.

A gang of skunks roams this prison yard with impunity and no one—and I mean no one—messes with them, not even the cats. One day, I watched a skunk walk through a group of inmates and they respectfully moved out of the way to let him pass. I was about to meet plenty of real gangsters during my stay here in federal prison, but I had just met a real OG—an original gangster.

As I began my stay here, I began meditating for long hours at a time. The inmates in my unit were amused and it became the talk of the complex. I remember running into ATL at the cafeteria one day, and he said, "Word is out that you meditate all day and all night." We laughed and I told him I was going to catch up on as much of it as I could while I had the time. But another inmate took notice for other reasons. He was a Native American called Nunaz who was in very good shape and very spiritual. One day, he approached me and said, "I see you're meditating. That's good.

Remember, you have to forget the outside world while you are here." Nunaz knew what he was talking about. He had been here ten years working on his thirty-year sentence. But he is always in good spirits and is as physically strong as he is mentally. Every week, he and the other Native Americans here engage in an interesting meditation. They set up a teepee, place hot coals inside, and take turns meditating inside the teepee. Nunaz explained to me that it is like entering the womb again and having a rebirth. I have many "professors" here, but Nunaz has become my spiritual guide for lack of a better title.

Fight Party

There are a lot of different factions here, and each of the different factions are referred to as "cars." The term "car" is not short for cartel, but rather a slang expression of who you ride with. Most of the "cars" here are separated along racial lines. There're black cars, white cars, hispanic cars, and there is even sex offender cars. At the cafeteria, you can tell segregation is alive and well because it's rare you see races or "cars" dine together. Some cars are made of geography, where inmates from the same city form a car. Of course, there are various gang members that link up with members of their prospective gangs. Each car has a head, and the heads are responsible for the discipline of the members of their cars if they get out of control. This is especially true if they get out of hand with a member of another car which could start a riot or war.

Even though they called the prison here a "low" security facility, the inmates here are far from being low-security inmates. The Federal Bureau of Prison—known better as the BOP—has a system where inmates can work their way down the ladder from high to medium to low based on a point system of their behavior, regardless of their charges. They can also work their way up the ladder as well. Some of the inmates I am locked up with are serving hard time, up to thirty years or more. One of the inmates here has shot a cop. Another inmate here has killed a cop. He and I continue to have very insightful conversations.

I found out quickly that it is true that my unit is considered the worst unit on the entire compound and that the most violent inmates are in here. I have and continue to witness fights that sometimes take on the atmosphere of a fight party. One night, I was invited to a slap party. What really impresses me about M-B is that no one in this unit has been stabbed since I have been here. The losers get their ass kicked without complaint like men are supposed to, and afterward, a cleaning crew mops up the blood before the guards arrive—if they come at all. We are locked in here by ourselves with no cameras and are unmonitored unless a guard decides to walk through and patrol. We are pretty much in here on our own and anything goes. If someone is beaten unconscious, like one inmate in another unit was, they will not get found until a guard walks through. That inmate was thrown in the laundry basket, so he was not found until count time.

Only once thus far have I seen an inmate pull a shank on another inmate in this unit, and I watched the orderly step to him and tell him to put the shank away or he would get put out. I observed our orderly, Wild Wild, run our unit like he's the sheriff. For all intent and purpose, he is the sheriff here. He ultimately decides who stays or has to leave the unit. Just like I used to tell violent criminals to leave "my county," if he told you to leave, you have to go to the guards and tell them to check you into isolation. If you do not, his soldiers will appear and kick your ass real good to make you go to the guards and beg them to take you out. It had been a long time since I had been around this level of testosterone. I wasn't even sure if this type of testosterone still existed, but it does, and it rejuvenates me every day.

The Lion's Den

I was in the bathroom shaving, when a very tall inmate with tattoos all over his body and face started a conversation. "Mr. Hill, if you ever need a haircut, let me know. I'm not going to judge you because you were a cop." Then he really surprised me. "Why don't you come to church Sunday? I am going to be giving my testimony." I love hearing a good sermon, so I agreed. It turned out that during his more-than-fourteen years in federal prison, not only had he found the Lord, he had decided to become a preacher. He not only invited me to a church service, but also invited me to nightly Bible study that goes on right after count. The spiritual leader of this group is Fabio, a Columbian who was on his nineteenth year serving a twenty-three-year prison term. Some of the most profound sermons I have ever heard were preached by Fabio at this Bible study. Fabio has become a great friend and pastor to me.

At the Bible study, one of the inmates asked for a prayer petition for an inmate who just arrived in our unit. He said the new inmate was terrified and afraid to take a shower or go to sleep. The inmate requesting prayer for the new inmate said the scared inmate felt he had been "thrown into a lion's den." Another inmate commented, "He *has* been thrown into the lion's den. This is a unit where all the violent 'problem children' are sent to."

After we prayed and left, I told my cellmate and a couple of his friends what was said at Bible study. They hurriedly agreed with what the new terrified inmate said about our housing unit being "the lion's den." One of them, who was a medical doctor before being sent to prison, said he was trying to get transferred upstairs because there were too many thugs here for him. He had been robbed by a gang of thugs before my arrival. He suggested I should try to get transferred with him. I told him I was having way too much fun watching the fights to go somewhere else at this point and be bored. One of them asked me why administration would assign me to a unit like this, knowing I was a cop.

"It was probably done on purpose," I replied. "But I like the atmosphere because it forces me to keep my edge like my job did, which—in a strange way—makes me feel at home."

They laughed and then one said, "I'm sure you do because you fit in well with these thugs. I guess throwing another lion in a lion's den is just a family reunion. Maybe you have found your long-lost brothers." He was being funny and elicited more laughter, but it would turn out he was right.

A month later, I was called up to the commander's office. When I walked in, he greeted me and got right to it. "I understand you are high profile and a high-ranking ex-law enforcement official. Is anyone giving you any problems?"

"Not at all," I replied.

"How is your family?" he followed up.

"They are fine," I replied.

Then he asked, "Well, how are you emotionally? Do you need any mental health assistance?"

"No, sir, I'm fine, but thanks for asking," I replied. An awkward silence filled the room. He did not know what to say from that point. I left and went back to the lion's den.

Honor Among Thieves

Even criminals are tough on crime. This is a concept not readily understood. Criminals do not like living in high-crime areas. There were known criminals who stayed in Clayton County while dealing crime in other counties because they knew their rivals would fear coming to strike back at them in "my county" while I was sheriff. They did not want to live in an environment where they did not feel safe either. They did not want their homes burglarized, their cars stolen, or to be robbed. The same holds true here in federal prison. If a thief is found in the midst here in the M-B unit, when they are identified, they are beaten severely and forced to go to guards to check themselves into isolation. Whenever there is any issue in the unit, the inmates here police it themselves, and they police well. They do not call the guards for anything except medical treatment.

One day, my tablet was stolen. I did not report it to the guards. I made a "police report" with the orderly/sheriff and was told it would be investigated. Three days later, while attending Bible study, I heard a man being chased while screaming for his life. He ran and beat on the doors screaming for the guards to come rescue him. They did and he had to be checked into solitary confinement for his safety immediately. When I walked back to my cell, my tablet was on my bed.

I have watched several thieves get their asses kicked and told to check themselves into solitary confinement. I only saw one man spared a beating because he was special needs. However, he was still told to leave and that he would not be spared if he did not. He checked himself the next day.

The inmates here in this unit police themselves so well, they do it better than the guards ever could. They even police for the guards. One day, an inmate began masturbating in front of a female guard. She called for backup, and they came and searched his cell, promising he would be written up. Ten minutes after the guards left, two "soldiers" walked into the inmate's cell and kicked his ass really good. The orderly/sheriff came and stopped it, saying that it was enough and told the inmate to go check himself in. The inmate started packing up while a clean-up crew came to mop up the blood. After the inmate went and checked himself in, the guards came to check to see if they could find out who beat him but could not find any bruises or cuts on anybody's hands, or anyone to volunteer information.

There was another violent incident here that really exemplifies "the honor among thieves." One day, while playing chess with one of my chess instructors, I saw several members of the Mexican car walking briskly, and they were all gloved up. The Mexicans are the most violent car in the unit and any time they glove up, everyone knows what time it is. It wasn't long before I could hear the familiar sound of flesh striking flesh and bones hitting bones. When it was done, the victim walked out bloodied, packed up his belongings, and went to see the guards to have himself checked in. Later, I found out he had been contacting another inmate's wife, telling her he would be out before her husband to take care of her sexually. When this reached the head of the Mexican car, he gave the order to have him punished and banished. Sad to say, I have never seen this type of honor in my chosen profession.

Even though the M-B housing unit is a violent place to be, it is the safest unit on the compound because of the way the inmates police themselves under Wild Wild's leadership. As long as I am here in prison, I have no desire to be transferred anywhere else. I am a fan of Wild Wild's leadership. But what I should have thought to ask myself early on is why am I still allowed to stay in M-B untouched when so many others are not. The answer is unbelievable.

The Untouchable

One day, an inmate told me he was amazed at how well I am received among the inmate population. He said he had never seen a cop interacting in prison with such ease in the eleven years he had been here. He added that the only prisoners held lower than child molesters were cops, and he was not expecting things to go well for me after my arrival.

I really did not understand the depths of what he was saying. I naively thought it was just because I was a likable guy and trained politician. I was used to interacting and communicating successfully with any and every one, to include a Klansman I discovered was still in Clayton County. The truth was my ability to build rapport with people was far from the sole reason why everyone became so friendly and left me alone. I soon found out there was a whole lot more politics going on behind the scenes than I knew.

ATL, the former drug lord from Atlanta who had introduced himself to me on my first day at the prison, was going to bat for me when it was being discussed how I should be dealt with. It turned out he had family members who lived in Clayton County. This former drug lord actually spoke on my behalf and told the inmates who did not like my presence that in Clayton County I was something of a Robin Hood-type figure who was beloved by his family and the people there. He told them that from what he could tell after researching my case, it appeared to him to be a political hit job. ATL said his family would know if I was truly a "bad cop" or not and told everyone they felt safer when I was the sheriff. ATL was the first to put the word out that any moves against me should be aborted.

Wild Wild did not come on board with this immediately. He took his time to observe me and research my case. Wild Wild is a very interesting and different type of gangster. Wild Wild is serving his seventeenth year on a twenty-one-year sentence for bank robbery. He is very well read, and it is rare you don't see a book in his hand. Once Wild Wild made up his mind that I was okay, there were no bones made about it because here, his word is unquestioned.

One day, while I was out in the yard, Wild Wild told one of his lieutenants that if anyone stepped to me, he was to handle it. Before I became aware of all of this and saw it with my own eyes, I was oblivious. As a result of these two bosses and another kingpin from Atlanta I would soon meet, everyone backed down. All of them became individuals I would come to develop unique relationships with, and they have become my "professors." I do not doubt just being seen with them was an unspoken signal I was to be left alone. When I am out and about walking with Wild Wild, it is like walking around with a celebrity. He reminds me a lot of a sheriff I once knew. How ironic that after years of being in politics and making many so-called friends in high places, it would be having "friends in low places" that would really matter.

Jailhouse Lawyers

Friends in low places would prove to be even more valuable than just muscle for protection. Wild Wild and ATL were very interested in my case and wanted me to appeal it. Both thought my case was bogus because they had seen the restraint chair used throughout their time in prison in much worse ways in the federal system, and never knew of anyone being indicted and sent to prison over it. They referred me to see a group of "legal experts" who might arguably be some of the best legal minds around who spent every day at the library. One of them was an inmate named Dracula. Every day, Dracula and a group of other legal minds got together and researched cases and wrote briefs. It was interesting to let them read over my case and get their thoughts on it. After all, these were inmates, and I am here for allegedly violating the rights of inmates, so I could not wait to see what they had to say. Another one of them was an inmate named Prince. Prince was a former member of the Nation of Islam and learned martial arts while serving as an FOI. Prince and I became sparring partners and began to play an interesting game where we would sneak up and ambush each other to test our situational awareness. Prince had been in the safety restraint chair many times during the twenty-six years he served in prison of which five were spent on death row. One time, he said he was kept in the restraint chair for sixteen hours. He took a special interest in my case and did a lot of research.

After they read over the case, they all could not believe the case was allowed to go forward to trial by the judge after reading the motion to dismiss filed by Lynsey Barron. I had to explain to them the politics behind how it all got started and how the judge was friends with the Clayton DA and an old political opponent of mine. They were very impressed by everything they read from Lynsey Barron. I told them she was handling my appeal and they wanted to be on Barron's research team, volunteering to help research case law to send her. Almost all these inmates had been in the safety restraint chair at certain times during their prison experience over the years. How ironic that inmates would disagree with me being prosecuted for the use of the safety restraint chair and volunteer to help with my representation.

My trips to the library would put me in touch with another gangster I never thought I would meet in this lifetime—"The General."

The General

One day, Dracula told me to be at the library at one p.m. sharp because he had a friend who really wanted to meet me. I thought nothing of it and said sure. When I arrived the next morning, I was met by a middle-aged, very business-like gentleman who shook my hand and greeted me warmly. "So, I finally get to meet the legendary Victor Hill," he said.

We both laughed and I said, "You must be from Atlanta."

"Not from there, but I have been there a long time."

"What part of Atlanta did you stay in?" I asked.

"I lived in Buckhead," he said, and the conversation continued from there, lasting over two hours. We enjoyed talking about the same people we either knew or knew of and the Atlanta experience. We talked a lot about real estate and politics but mostly about the stock market. We did not talk about why he or I were in federal prison for a while, until one day, it came up when we were discussing crime in Atlanta and the unconventional tactics I used to run drug dealers out of Clayton County came up. He agreed with the way I handle drugs and said it was the way it should be handled, but he slipped and said something that made me realize trafficking drugs was why *he* was there. I went and researched the man I had been talking to every day for the last two weeks and realized I had befriended perhaps the biggest drug trafficker in Atlanta since Big Meech from the black Mafia family.

At our next meeting, I confronted him of course. "So, you were the 'Ghost Kingpin' of Atlanta I didn't get to catch, huh?"

He laughed. "Actually, I was a businessman who diversified, and one of my businesses just happened to be drugs. I was more like the chairman of the board."

"Okay, Mr. Chairman," I said as we both laughed out loud. Now that we fully knew and understood where each of us was coming from, the conversations got better and more intense. Usually, we meet in the yard after the General's morning run and we would go at it about politics and crime, but it would always end up back on the stock market. The General was very knowledgeable about the stock markets, especially commodities and futures, and expanded my knowledge on them weekly. I also learned that the General was also the third vote on the board of why I was left alone because he also put the word out that I was not to be touched.

The General also does a lot of legal research and showed interest in my case. It is interesting that he and all the inmates who research my case agree with how I ran the jail and used the safety restraint chair. You would think it would be the exact opposite, but it is not. Once the General read my appeal, he was convinced my case should be overturned, but often warned it may have to go as high as the Supreme Court to get away from all the politics surrounding me. The people who know our polar-opposite backgrounds and saw us walking and talking all the time are intrigued and some seem confused. I'm sure they wonder what the former head of a law enforcement agency and a former Atlanta drug kingpin could possibly have to talk about. But no one dared to cross the line to find out which led to much speculation across the compound. Most who watch our interactions think we are plotting on how we can join forces and rule over Atlanta, Georgia, when we get out. Nothing could be further from the truth about my friendship and conversations with the General. The General has turned out to be a man of great faith and preaches to me consistently about why we should always keep faith in God in all circumstances, because as he hammers to me almost every day, "God always has a plan." He also talks a lot about how the time he has wasted being loyal to the streets has taught him there is no love or loyalty in the streets, ultimately taking you from the family you love. The General says he has no more time to give the prison system.

Training Day

Many here believe I am some type of mob-type figure from Atlanta because of the stories that have circulated here. Often while conversing with inmates, my past of being the sheriff comes up in conversation. Mostly out of curiosity with many questions. Some of the younger inmates will come get me anytime they find a rap song that mentions me in the lyrics. To my surprise, they found a rapper, BEO Lil Kenny, out of Memphis, who had mentioned me in his rap song, "Good Love," a month after my arrival at federal prison. They also found two more new underground raps that came out since my arrival, and they have listened to the ones that came before. They also introduced me to a famous rapper serving time here called Rio Da Yung OG, who is a very good rapper. I hate disappointing the youth, so I neither confirm nor deny, but I listen intently to the very interesting mythical stories that get imported here from their contacts in Atlanta. Although I am well protected by the head of the vice lords and two other bosses, even they believe their job was made easier by the mythical reputation that preceded me before my arrival.

I briefly got a job tutoring in the library and met another tutor, Mike Money, who teaches classes on creative writing. I signed up for his class because I thought it would be interesting. Mike Money is an author and has already authored several books. I also met another author who I became good friends with called One Hundred Shades of Gray. I ordered Mike Money's and One Hundred Shade's books to get a sample of their work. Mike Money was serving time for bank robbery. Bank robbers are held in high esteem here in prison because they are considered to be the most daring breed of criminals. I remember one time; I was in a class with him when he started describing how he had robbed one particular bank. When he started speaking, you would have thought E. F. Hutton had been raised from the dead because everyone stopped what they were doing and literally leaned their ears toward him to listen to the details. They were fascinated, and so was I.

As my conversations with Mike Money continued over time, my past life became part of much discussion as well. Mike said when I first arrived, he was in the yard and overheard some other inmates referring to me as the real-life "Training Day." When the other inmates in our discussion group heard this, they all burst out in laughter.

One said, "All right, Mr. Training Day."

From that moment on, my nickname became, "Training Day." When one of the books, *Rules to the Game*, Mike Money authored arrived, he autographed it for me, addressing me as "Training Day." No one truly escapes getting a nickname here.

I enjoyed reading Mike Money's books. He is a great writer of urban novels, and his work is authentic because he has lived that life. Mike made an interesting suggestion to me one day. Mike said, since I was still receiving "honorable mentions" in gangster rap songs, I should take advantage of the misconception that I am some type of gangster cop like the one portrayed by Denzel Washington in Training Day. Mike suggested I should consider letting him write a fictional book using my "urban myth persona" as the main character. As financially promising as Mike's idea sounded, I explained to him that in Atlanta, we have a lot of Robert Ford Syndrome prosecutors and one of them has even started targeting and indicting rappers for their lyrics. I further explained that if a book came out using my name as a fictional crime boss, the DA in my county and federal prosecutors would team up again to make up another ham sandwich indictment. Mike found my reply humorous, but I was dead serious and reminded him about how I got here. Mike replied, suggesting I write a nonfiction book about my case instead.

"Maybe when I get some time," I said.

"You will never have more time than you have now," he replied.

"You might be right about that," I replied and did not give it another thought.

Fight for Us

At the nightly scripture prayer circle, the ministering took a different twist that caught me completely off guard one night.

The second lead preacher in this Bible study next to Fabio is Scooter. I enjoy listening to them both. In the middle of his sermon on this occasion, "Reverend Scooter" called me out and said, "I understand you lived a privileged life before you came here." Everyone busted out in laughter.

"I did," I replied, wondering where this was going.

"You do realize you were sent here for a reason, right?"

I said nothing while waiting to hear what he thought the reason possibly could be, other than what I knew it to be. Reverend Scooter went on saying, "You were sent here to see the truth of how we are mistreated and victimized by an unfair system and the filthy conditions under which we live. You are going to fight for us by becoming our voice."

I did not reply. I just nodded in bewilderment.

The next day at the library, I told Mike Money about what was said in the prayer circle. "Now is the time to write the book," he insisted. "Don't wait until you get out, write it now while you are still here so the world will know the real story of how you got here and what happens here."

I knew he was right, but I really wasn't mentally up to the task for all the work it takes to write every day. I was not a fan of term papers when I was in school, and this would be the longest-term paper I would ever have to write. I had developed a daily routine schedule that consisted of meditation, chess, dominos, and poker, which made my days interesting and time fly. I also enjoyed taking breaks to go to the library to dialogue with my "professors." I knew writing this book would bring all of that to a halt, and it did. The following is what my "professors" want the world to hear, and I am honored to be their voice.

Real Criminal Justice Reform

During my time here, at the federal pen, I have had many discussions with the inmates about what's wrong with the criminal justice system that I can corroborate through my personal experience. I've got to see first-hand what happens in the criminal justice system from the grand jury process to the court and trial process, and ultimately to the prison where I now am. The inmates here and I have had deep discussions on what needs to be fixed in the system to make it fair for all. What they are suggesting is not only reasonable, but it also makes sense.

I know first-hand that innocent people can and do go to prison.

I know first-hand that no matter what the law says or how case law is worded, there are judges who write rulings that contradict how they have ruled in the past for others. I also know first-hand that a prosecutor who wants to prosecute someone can find creative ways to make a case on anyone they want to see go to prison. However, most of the inmates I have engaged in dialogue with here admitted they were guilty of crimes and should have been prosecuted. Their complaint is *how* they were prosecuted and over-sentenced, sometimes given far more time than others who had committed far worse crimes. The following are issues they want to give voice to, hoping it will perhaps reach ears that would not otherwise hear their pleas for justice.

Grand Jurys

If we want to talk about something that will forever put doubt in the minds of legal philosophers, that would be our grand jury system. Under our current criminal justice system, we are supposed to have the right to face our accusers, but the grand jury system in our country does not give people that right. Imagine, any prosecutor can walk into a room of twelve people, provide free coffee and Chick-fil-A lunches to them, and can tell them whatever he wants to about a defendant without him being present with counsel to defend himself. There is no legal representation for the defendant to present to grand jurors why he may be innocent. This allows prosecutors to skip the process of having to meet the elements of a crime by having to obtain a warrant from a judge, bypassing the scrutiny of a legal eye to see if the probable cause and elements of a crime exist. A prosecutor can tell unsuspecting jurors not trained in the specific elements of law whatever he wants and leave out whatever facts he thinks will not help him get an indictment. If by chance the prosecutor lies to the grand jury, there are no checks and balances or repercussions for them doing so. Because of the unfair grand jury process, prosecutors can put charges on almost anyone for anything, putting them in a bad legal and financial situation. The grand jury process allows prosecutors to intimidate over 90 percent of the defendants they indict into some type of plea deal.

In a system that claims you have a right to face your accusers and claims you have the right to defend yourself against charges, the grand jury process is probably the most egregious violation of one's constitutional rights in our criminal justice system. Especially when you put it in the hands and control of prosecutors who use it for political purposes and think nothing of lying to a grand jury because of the lack of checks and balances to hold them accountable for their lies.

If we wonder why the system is backlogged with cases and the jails are overcrowded, look no further than the grand jury process. Fix this, and the domino effect will be powerfully positive. Until this is fixed, the prison will be filled with people not necessarily guilty. Prosecutors mainly rely on the fact that if they can get a person indicted, it is likely they will take a plea. More than 90 percent of the people who are indicted do exactly just that. The prison is full of people who took plea deals because prosecutors went through unfair processes to indict them many times without sufficient evidence that would probably never have met the mustard in a full-blown trial.

If we truly want to reform the criminal justice system and make it fair for all, the grand jury system must be revised, if not done away with altogether. It is still the closest thing to a kangaroo court in a country that is supposed to have the best and most fair legal system in the world. Even if the grand jury is not done away with, the best reform would be to give everyone the opportunity to be present before the grand jury, with their counsel to give them the opportunity to defend themselves instead of prosecuting them in a star chamber.

Plea Deals

Plea deals are part of what prosecutors, especially the federal government, brag about when they say they have a high conviction rate. The truth of the matter is most of their convictions are done because of plea deals. And make no mistake, nine times out of ten, a prosecutor will hold a "plea gun" to the defendant's head, threatening he will get more time if he goes to trial. If they offer you five years if you take a plea deal, why do you get ten years if you exercise your constitutional rights to go to trial and you lose? Is this not punishment for exercising your constitutional right?

Some public defenders help force plea deals so they don't have to do the actual trial work since they are government-paid workers. Many defendants are amazed though at how much they pay attorneys, only to have them talk them into taking plea deals with the threat of serving more time.

Prosecutors often stack and put the highest charge they can on a defendant in indictments even though the elements of what the person did do not fit the highest charge. They do this to convince them to take a plea while lying to them that they are getting a bargain when they are not. For example, if a person is guilty of involuntary manslaughter, why should they be indicted on murder charges when they didn't intend on killing anybody? It is no different than a retailer marking up the price and then giving the illusion they're taking the price down when they're selling it for what they were intended to do in the first place. This is not right and is unjustly unfair.

If these tactics truly work to serve the purpose of reducing crime, then crime should be low all over the country but it's not. The only purpose it truly serves is for the prosecutors to get a win for their stats or to get them their fifteen seconds of fame at a press conference. If everyone truly has a constitutional right to a trial, punishing them with more time if they do not take a plea deal is wrong. I never thought the day would come when I would quote a mob boss, but as I talk to the inmates here, I am reminded of a documentary I once saw on John Gotti where he told his son that if everyone would stop taking plea deals, the jails would be empty. He may well have been right about that one.

Over Sentencing

The over-sentencing and inconsistency in sentencing that goes on in our criminal justice system is another travesty. Do not, for one second, misinterpret that I am now soft on crime. I am not and never will be, but the amount of time some of the inmates around me are serving is ridiculous and does nothing to reduce crime outside while costing taxpayers an astronomical amount of money to keep them here. Perhaps there is something to the conspiracy theory we have heard about keeping people incarcerated because it's a billion-dollar industry, but that's not what I'm getting at here.

As I have stated earlier, the best way to control drugs is to control the territory. That way, drug dealers are simply unable to sell drugs. But if you lock up a drug dealer or drug lord and give him thirty years in jail, it does not slow down or put a dent in drug trafficking at all. I am currently incarcerated with men serving twenty- and thirty-year sentences for trafficking drugs, some of whom avoided "my county" because they knew they could not operate there.

I know for a fact the distribution of drugs has not changed at all in the outside world. It is alive and well here at this prison. When you lock up the head drug dealer in the neighborhood, there are five more waiting in line to take his place. If giving someone a life sentence for selling drugs was effective, we should have little to no drugs in this county. We all know this is not the case. The true purpose prison is supposed to serve is to keep violent, dangerous people away from society so they can't kill or injure anyone. However, locking up people for committing financial crimes for long periods of time doesn't really serve a purpose and it does not help their victims either. I believe their victims would better enjoy people who commit financial crimes against them being made to work jobs with 50 percent of their income going to pay restitution to them instead. If these people are not an immediate threat to society, this is a better way to get justice for their victims. When we lock up people for exuberant periods of time, we begin running an extremely costly, convalescent home when they begin aging at the expense of taxpayers. If inmates are so old they can't take care of themselves, how can they possibly be a danger to others?

Also, sentencing across the country is very inconsistent. There are people here serving thirty years who had no physical contact with their victims and others not serving half of that who did have physical and violent contact. These inmates are not saying they should not be here, they are questioning how long they are here as opposed to those who have done far worse.

One inmate made a very interesting suggestion in our insight-ful dialogues. He said judges, prosecutors, and cops should spend a week in prison so they can have a better understanding of what they are sentencing people to. He suggested this would not weaken them on crime but strengthen their knowledge to make better decisions about who should be imprisoned and how long they should be there. He went on to say this could cause them to focus more on those who pose a threat to the safety of others. Per-haps those with the Robert Ford Syndrome could benefit from this the most.

High Paying Jobs

There are paying jobs you can get while in prison. When I first got to federal prison, I decided to look for a job to keep myself occupied before my full-time job became writing this book. Some inmates recommended I go to the library and become an instructor and teach classes. There was a shortage of instructors so, with a recommendation, I got hired easily. The fact it was a paid position sounded great. I thought, perhaps I could save for the new luxury car I was planning on buying once I got out. However, when I found out I was going to be paid eighteen cents an hour, I pretty much realized I was going to have to find other financial resources instead.

This has come up in many dialogues with the inmates here.

They make a very valid point by asking if we have passed minimum wage laws, why does it not apply to them? If minimum wage is thirteen dollars an hour, how can we justify paying someone eighteen cents just because they are an inmate convicted of committing a crime? How do we expect people willing to work a full eight-hour day to make a living to support their families back home or save money so they can go and be the productive citizens in society we demand them to be with eighteen cents an hour? I don't think anyone in their right mind could possibly think this is fair and I do not disagree with them on this. They are already paying their debt to society for the crimes they have committed by serving time, so why can they not be paid like anybody else if they are willing to work for it? They are not asking for six figures, just minimum wage. That is very reasonable and not too much to ask.

Loss of Rights for Convicted Felons

In a society that claims we want people to exit prison and be productive citizens, the legislation we allow to be created conflicts with this lofty theory. If this is what we truly desire, changes need to be made. We, as a society, say we don't understand why when convicted felons get out of jail, they can't just go get a job like everyone else, yet we set in place a system that makes it difficult—if not close to impossible—for them to do so. We prevent convicted felons from being doctors, lawyers, and a host of anything special because they must be punished for the rest of their lives for their sins, even after they've served time *to pay* for their crimes.

Yet when we invite them to church, we tell them they are forgiven if they just confess their sins to the Lord. The Lord does forgive, but as a society, we do not. There are some states that go as far as not allowing convicted felons to have a barber's license—yet our society wonders why they can't just go get a job. Political enemies who are prosecutors or have relationships with them use this flaw in our criminal justice system as a tool to convict their political opponents if they feel they can't defeat them at the polls. Ask me how I know. If you get convicted of anything, you can't work here, you can't go there, you can't vote, you cannot run for office, and you can't ever carry a gun again. Did I say carry a gun?

Perhaps the most interesting dialogue I have had with inmates here at the Forrest City Federal Correctional Center is about their right to bear arms after becoming convicted felons. This has turned into a very spirited debate since one of my main strategies as sheriff for controlling violent crime was taking guns out of the hands of violent criminals. But I must confess, they are winning some parts of this ongoing debate with good reason. Their logic is if a person has been convicted of a violent crime, especially one dealing with a firearm, they can see why they would no longer be permitted to have a weapon. However, if they are convicted of a nonviolent crime like tax fraud, why could they never go quail hunting again or at least have a weapon at home to protect their families? They have vehemently expressed to me that, whether I agree or not or how I choose to interpret it, the Constitution gives everyone the right to bear arms.

I still believe people who have committed violent crimes should not be in possession of firearms. Common sense dictates that individuals who have shot people in the commission of felonies should not be in possession of them. However, I can't say I am convinced nonviolent offenders should be denied this right after hearing their arguments. This debate continues and is ongoing as I write this section.

The Compelling Irony

It was a belief of the people who plotted to send me to this prison that the inmates here would hate me for restraining inmates I knew had the potential for violence. It was their hope I would be forced to serve my time in solitary confinement for my safety. As these inmates researched and found out more about my case, they instead became advocates for my cause, contributed suggestions for my appeal, and encouraged me to go to the highest court if necessary due to the politics surrounding my case. They demanded I write this book while contributing to its content and editing. Many of my "professors" have been in the safety restraint chair themselves and still cannot believe the feds have prosecuted me for what they have seen as standard procedures in many of the federal prisons. The irony is compelling.

I am only a few days away from being released from prison as I finish writing this book. I have already begun gathering the prison art I have collected here to get it all packed up. One is a knitted mask of the cowl of the fictional vigilante I have often been compared to—yes, a Batman mask. The inmate who made it and gave it to me said he wanted me to have it in case the need ever arises for me to have to wear it again. The irony. Another inmate gave me a wooden medallion where he carved out and painted the image of a lion to symbolize that I was walking out of their lion's den, undevoured. Over the years, I have received badges for bravery and courage, but none do I hold in as much high esteem as this medallion.

Here, I have bonded with a group of men I spent the last thirty years of my life hunting and incarcerating. Now they have become my professors, supporters, political consultants, chess coaches, martial arts instructors, editors for this book, and yes, a lot of them are now my friends.

Does life imitate art or does art imitate life?

As I ask this philosophical question my mind wanders to the last movie in the Dark Knight trilogy, *The Dark Knight Rises*. In that movie, after the villain Bane breaks Batman's back, he imprisons him with inmates in a very deep pit where legend has it, only one has ever been able to make the extremely deadly climb out of the pit to freedom. The irony was the inmates not only helped Batman recover from his back injury, but helped coach and cheer him on to make the climb out of the pit so he could return to Gotham and fight Bane again.

Once he finally made the climb to escape the pit of life imprisonment, he stopped when he found some rope long enough to help them get out of the pit and threw it down to assist them in getting their freedom too.

I sincerely hope this book will be the proverbial rope I throw back into the pit, here, in the Forest City Federal Prison that will help all those here who helped me, with some knowing that—with the number of years they have been sentenced to—they may not live long enough to ever see freedom again.

Epilogue

T hroughout this book, I have put the words "my county" in quotation marks to make a point. The press and prosecutors used this saying when I told criminals to "stay out of my county," to paint a picture that I thought Clayton was *my* county in an arrogant and illegal way. The leadership school of extreme owner-ship teaches that good and powerful leadership is about taking ownership of *everything* in the leader's purview. I will always refer to Clayton County as my county because, as its leader, I took ownership of everything that happened there, good or bad. And I just didn't take mere ownership, I took extreme ownership. That's what leaders are supposed to do. Clayton County is my county and always will be. I did what was needed to protect my county, and it *was* a safe place because of it.

The Aftermath Domino Effect

Jeff Turner ultimately lost the election for sheriff to the person I helped get in office before I went to prison. Comically, even after I withdrew my support for this individual after I saw the misuse of budget and personnel and supported a third party instead, Turner still could not win the election against this candidate. After all the planning and plotting done by Turner and DA Tasha Mosley to have me indicted, convicted, and sent to prison, they still could not get him elected sheriff and could not even get who they wanted elected to fill his seat as chairman or another open seat in a commission district. That gave me a good laugh on election night and put a bigger smile on my face than the one I had on the plane the day I left. But when I woke up, I realized I was laughing at the domino effect caused by these two dummies that had cost people their lives. I stopped smiling and laughing out of respect for the lives that have been and will continue to be lost.

My political prosecution, gave the criminals in Clayton County a huge victory from our judicial system they are enjoying to the fullest at the cost of lives in the jail and on the streets. Four inmates have been murdered at the Clayton County Jail. No one was murdered at the jail during my fourteen years as sheriff due to my methods of using nonviolent tools as the safety restraint chair to control violent criminals. In addition, another inmate who was trying to commit suicide was accidentally killed by officers who held him down too long to prevent him from jumping off of the top tier of the housing unit. They held him down while the captain went looking for flex cuffs to restrain him since the restraint chair was not an option due to my prosecution. The inmate died from suffocation of the weight of the officers on top of him. Numerous stabbings have now become the norm, and some inmates have taken to extorting inmates' families, threatening harm to their loved ones if they are not paid ransom money via Cash App. Assaults on officers increased immensely and even a civilian nurse was slapped by an inmate. Many employees, especially civilians, are now fearful to work in the jail and many resigned, expressing their fears in their resignation letters. Knowing the current administration is fearful to use any lawful means to control them, the inmates have taken total control of the jail.

They have also taken control of the streets. After my political prosecution, the violence trickled from the jail out to the streets and the murder rate didn't just go up, it went up to an all-time high in the county's history. Two of the restraint chair inmates I was accused of also have been emboldened by my prosecution to continue to take their aggression toward law enforcement to another level as well. Cleveland Jackson's new hobby is to put a dash cam video on his car and chase down officers he believes are speeding, while screaming at them to slow down. He also has gone back to walking up on them in an aggressive manner while filming their response. Whenever he does this, he can count on getting a spot on the six o'clock news to support his aggressive conduct toward officers.

Glen Howell recently saw Officer Guthrie (the officer whom he tore up his yard and ran his girlfriend off the road) at a gas station and verbally assaulted him while walking up on him after having to be told numerous times to step back. In both cases, the officers were hesitant to act because they knew the media and prosecutors can and will turn the situation around on them as they have done on me.

Prosecutors were so enthralled with the idea of coming after me, that they either did not anticipate or perhaps care about the danger they were putting inmates, officers, and civilian lives, both in the jail and on the streets.

In addition to the dangerous threat posed to anyone these types of prosecutors decide to target, the domino effect of their misuse of the criminal justice system continues to trickle down to the streets everywhere, perpetuating the crime situation our nation now faces. I'm not saying we should let police officers get away with any legitimate wrongdoing. However, when we allow media-hungry prosecutors to pursue them with "creative" prosecution for what they were legally trained to do just to make a name for themselves or control elections, officers are going to continue to be terrified to do their jobs. When officers are terrified to do their jobs, it becomes a domino effect that leads to high crime, because criminals go unstopped and unchecked while law enforcement remains hesitant about what to say or do when they encounter them, so they simply do nothing at all.

Just like in third-world countries, rogue prosecutors are weaponizing the criminal justice system to imprison their declared political rivals more and more, with no checks and balances to hold them accountable. If we continue to allow prosecutors to present cases to grand juries without defense for the accused and allow them to lie to grand juries with impunity, we will never truly have a fair democratic form of government from our judicial system.

As previously stated, I will always wonder if the prosecutors, media, and judges who condemned my actions would still feel and rule the same if the violent individuals I authorized to be placed in the safety restraint chair for preventive measures had done to their family members what they did to their victims. The media often plays the video of me telling Joseph Arnold that he sounded like a jackass when he told me the reason he savagely beat up two elderly women in a grocery store was because they cut in front of him in line. They stopped playing the video that showed him beating them. They also frequently say I had a seventeen-year-old placed in the chair to give sympathy for his age, but do not show the video made by police when he vandalized his mother's house while destroying food for his infant sibling because she would not buy him higher speed internet. The judicial system, with the help of the media, has done an excellent job of making these violent individuals out to be pitied as poor little victims of an alleged "vigilante sheriff."

Interestingly, a police brutality podcast *Good Luck America* that watched the video of me speaking to Joseph Arnold was wondering and asking where the excessive force I used was. The podcaster actually spoke in my defense and ironically quoted Colonel Jessup, a character brilliantly portrayed by Jack Nicholson in the classic movie *A Few Good Men*. I appreciated the analogy of comparison in one sense, but must say what Colonel Jessup ordered resulted in a death. What I ordered only resulted in six violent men being restrained for safety for four hours while being checked every fifteen minutes by officers and nurses. However, this comparison did make me go back and revisit exactly what Colonel Jessup said in the movie. I decided to reword how it would read if I had to articulate it at my trial when being cross-examined by the federal prosecutor. It would read this way instead:

> *Here is the truth you can't handle. We live in a world of violence, and that world must be guarded by people with guns and badges. Who is going to do this? You? I have a greater responsibility than you can fathom. You weep for men who savagely beat elderly women in a grocery store, destroy their mother's home, run a woman off the road, and destroy the yard*

of a law enforcement officer, and curse me for it. You have that luxury. You have that luxury of not knowing what I know, that while these six men being restrained was tragically uncomfortable for them, it probably saved lives. And my existence, while grotesque and incomprehensible to you, saves lives! You don't want the truth because deep down, in places you don't talk about at parties, you want me standing in the gap, in that thin line between your family and violent criminals. You need me standing on that line. We use words like accountability and higher standards as the backbone of defending those who can't defend themselves. You use them as a punchline for political prosecutions. I have neither the time nor the inclination to explain myself to a man who sleeps and rises to the protection I provide, and then Monday morning quarterbacks the way I provide it with a novel theory of prosecution. I would rather you just say thank you and go on your merry way. Otherwise, I suggest you pick up a badge and gun and man a shift at the Clayton County Jail full of violent criminals who have already killed four inmates since your landmark "novel prosecution." Either way, I will always give a damn about the safety you have taken from law enforcement, making them even more unsure what they can and cannot do and how that will continue to place both their lives and the lives of inmates in danger.

The Lions of Nakuru Park

I remember sitting around, talking to my "professors" at the

Forest City Federal Prison about my case and the aftermath of crime and violence in the jail and streets of my county that was the result. One of the inmates, after listening, gave an interesting analogy. He asked if I had ever heard of what happened with the lions at Nakuru Park. I had not. He articulated that it turned out someone thought it would be a good idea to take the lions out of Nakuru Park after they had consumed a considerable amount of wildlife. However, this move turned into an ecological disaster. The wildlife was no longer kept in check by the lions. National Geographic said, "Without lions to keep other predators in check, their numbers and their boldness can explode, leading to greater human-wildlife conflicts." It turned out lions are needed to maintain the balance of nature.

With this analogy in mind at the point of this conclusion, the question must be asked, who is truly the vigilante? Is it the media who incite riots and attempt to influence the outcome of elections and verdicts by the omission of facts as well as the commission of lies? Is it the prosecutors who can lie to grand juries with impunity to indict their political enemies even when they have no clearly established case law of a criminal violation? Am I a vigilante? Or am I merely a proverbial lion that was following ecological state training and policy to balance the nature of crime? You be the judge.

Author's Note
Legal Update on United States vs. Victor Hill

A fter my release from federal prison on May 18, 2024, my case was heard orally by a panel of three on the Eleventh Circuit on April 16th. On April 29th, less than two weeks after hearing the arguments, three panel members of the Eleventh Circuit confirmed the convictions. Although the circuit is supposed to decide on law versus facts, they ruled on "facts" created by prosecutors and witnesses I had either fired, arrested, or both. My attorney argued law that dictates my case should have never gone before a jury, because according to case law in United States vs. Lanier, "the law should be sufficiently developed so it is clear the charged conduct falls within the statues scope." The law is supposed to "clearly establish" a crime with "obvious clarity" and be "beyond debate."

Even though the district judge stated, on record, this case was the first of its kind, the Eleventh Circuit compared my case to other cases involving an inmate being restrained to a hitching post in the hot sun, and restraint chair cases where the inmates were tazed, beaten, pepper sprayed, and in some cases, died as a comparison to my case where no physical force was used and inmates were attended to every fifteen minutes. They said these cases were clear in warning everyone that just putting someone in the restraint chair alone, if they are not violent at the time, is a felony crime. Their ruling also conflicted with other restraint case rulings the Eleventh

Circuit handed down in the past which said that "painful hand-cuffing, without more, is not excessive force in cases where the resulting injuries are minimal," and case law in this circuit "tends to indicate that the use of restraints is permissible." According to US vs. Lanier, if the law was anything short of being completely clear, the rule of lenity should apply. I can only conclude that the rule of lenity only applies to who they want it to, since I was shown no lenity and was the first in history to go to prison for something unestablished as illegal.

As far as the district judge calling out a holdout juror twice to question him, which the Eleventh Circuit panel said they had never seen before, only a concurring opinion strongly admonishing Judge Ross that this should not be done again was issued. We can only guess that since her actions were "a novel case of first impression," she was granted the rule of lenity that US vs. Lanier said should apply in cases like mine instead of granting me a mistrial. The case is being prepared to appeal at the next level.

Acknowledgments

I want to acknowledge my aunt, Audrey Pinckney, my uncle, Joseph Brown, and my brother, Jerome Hill, for all the support and encouragement they rendered during this undertaking.

A very special thank you to my best friend and brother Jarret Gorlin, and his father, Steve Gorlin, who took me in and treated me like one of his sons. This book would not have happened without them.

Appendix of Restraint Chair Cases

*2013, Georgia—Civil lawsuit, judge granted summary judgment, in favor of sheriff and employees. In one instance, the inmate's nose was broken while in the restraint chair. No FBI involvement, no federal grand jury, no federal indictment.

*2016, St. Louis—Inmate placed in restraint chair for five days in lieu of medical treatment while forced fed in chair, causing him to defecate on himself. Civil suit. No FBI involvement, no federal grand jury, no indictment.

*2016, Georgia—Sheriff sued for a man who died in a jail cell after brawl with deputies and strapped into a restraint chair. Civil lawsuit. No FBI involvement, no federal grand jury, no indictment.

*2018, Michigan—Inmate strapped in restraint chair and struck in the head several times by deputies, and tased in the groin. Federal civil rights lawsuit only. No FBI involvement, no federal grand jury, no indictment.

*2017, Tennessee—Inmate was tased while in restraint chair, resulting in civil lawsuit only. No FBI involvement, no federal grand jury, no indictment.

*2018, Wilke Barre—Inmate placed in restraint chair while tased and brutalized. Civil lawsuit only. No FBI involvement, no federal grand jury, no indictment.

*2023 Myric vs. Fulton County Atlanta—Inmate placed in restraint chair for resisting. After becoming compliant, remained in restraint chair and died. No FBI involvement, no federal grand jury, no indictment. Eleventh Circuit ruled qualified immunity.

About the Author

V ictor Hill served one term in the Georgia Legislature as a state representative before being elected sheriff, where he authored four bills that were passed into law. Hill served as sheriff for a total of fourteen years and is now retired, pursuing a new career as an author.